The Saucier's Apprentice

Raymond Sokolov

The Saucier's Apprentice

*A Modern Guide
to Classic French Sauces
for the Home*

*Alfred A. Knopf
New York   2011*

THIS IS A BORZOI BOOK
PUBLISHED BY ALFRED A. KNOPF, INC.

Library of Congress Cataloging in Publication Data

Sokolov, Raymond A.   The saucier's apprentice.

Includes index.
1. Sauces.   2. Cookery, French.   I. Title.
TX819.A1S64   1976   641.8′14   75–34281
ISBN 0–394–48920–9

Manufactured in the United States of America
Published March 29, 1976
Reprinted Eighteen Times
Twentieth Printing, August 2011

To my friends, who came to dinner with
"vino et sale et omnibus cachinnis"

Contents

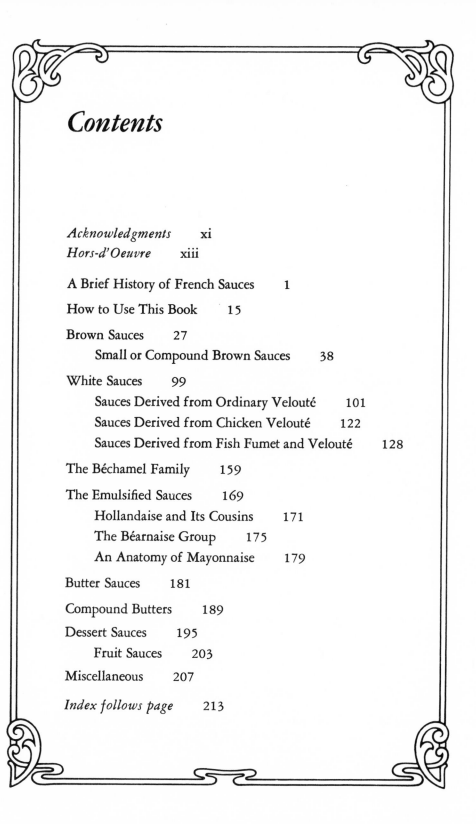

Genealogies

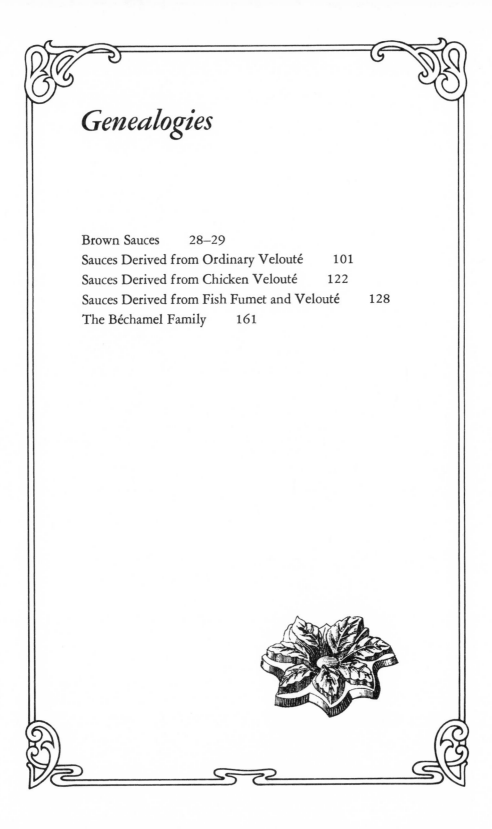

Acknowledgments

George Lang encouraged me at the beginning. My editor, Judith Jones, applauded the results of an early testing ordeal conducted under semi-tropical conditions in the New York summer heat; and then she continued to support the project with her well-known good taste and with friendly dollops of criticism. I am grateful to Earl Tidwell for his skillful work in designing the book. Sal's Market in Brooklyn Heights and the Fulton Retail Fish Market in Manhattan responded gallantly to some bizarre requests. E. Dehillerin, the legendary Parisian kitchenware concern, kindly permitted me to use illustrations from one of their antique catalogues.

Mainly, however, I want to thank Margaret, Michael, and Joseph for submitting to months of late dinners and to an enforced period of gastronomic time travel backwards into the nineteenth century.

Hors-d'Oeuvre

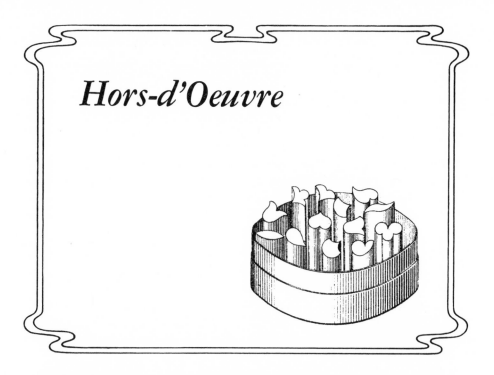

Having fled London and the odor of fried bread, I first set foot in France in the summer of 1960, famished from the boat train, unable to speak three words of the language, without maps or reservation, and a little terrified. Somehow I negotiated the Métro and found a phenomenally cheap and garish room in a Left Bank *hôtel garni*.

Settled in that small garret, at eye level with a forest of chimney pots and mansards, I attempted to repair the ravages of the Channel crossing and promptly burnt out my electric razor on the unexpectedly high Parisian voltage. I would grow a beard. I was nineteen. There wasn't time to shave. I was too hungry—for life, but mainly for dinner.

Down the oblate, winding stair, past the whiskered hag concierge and around the corner, they were waiting for me: a family of Basques with a cheap menu. Tournedos bordelaise could be had, "bleeding," as I learned to say, for the equivalent of $1.50.

That night, I knew enough to know that I had ordered some kind of steak. From bordelaise, I knew not.

I was, however, aware that the French distinguished their food with "sauces," but it was not until the little barded tournedos was brought, aswim in a lush and velvet medium, that I began to understand what had been meant by those groans of retrospective pleasure which the racy dowager next door to us in Detroit had emitted involuntarily as she regaled us with lengthy accounts of her unstinted banquets in Michelin's three-starred temples.

"Oh, the sauces!"

And, oh, that bordelaise of my first night in France. I am certain, now, that it must have been third-rate: padded with tomato, unskimmed and murky, chalky with raw flour. But I remember a taste of extreme purity, an excitement that, along with the thrill of mainlining the French language, held me captive in Paris for the next two months, impelled me to return to work there some years later, and has most recently produced the work at hand.

The point is that one sauce led to another. I have stopped counting them, for who but a drudge would want to keep records of any but the supreme (no pun intended): an earthy, witty choron *chez* Paul Bocuse; the startling and powerful brown sauce with charolais beef at Troisgros in Roanne; and its cousin, barbed slightly with pepper for the venison, at Illhaeusern.

Great chefs, it goes without saying, still continue the art of the *saucier,* the sauce chef. And we pay them in bundles for their efforts, because we agree (to paraphrase Brillat-Savarin) that a great meal without a sauce is like a beautiful woman without clothes. It can provoke and satisfy the appetite, but it lacks the coating of civilization that would arouse our fullest interest.

I know that there are people who say that raw materials of the highest order are the key to a good meal. I agree that a perfect peach is a fine thing, and I say also that the decline of the tomato in these United States vitiates the quality of what we eat beyond the rescue of a mere cook's ingenuity.

But there is another side (at least one) to this question. A cook can make a difference. A custard is more than the sum of its yolk and sugar parts. The play of the culinary intellect yields a palatable profit on the plate. And it is nonsense to say that complex results are not just as tasty and more *interesting* than simple ones. A sauce, in other words, adds something, really two things: a taste as well as the opportunity to think about how the thing was made. This is the same kind of pleasure we derive when we look at a painting; the eye is pleased, while the mind explores the esthetic windings of a technique and a willed structure.

French sauces are the height of culinary technique, as anyone who has made a hollandaise already knows. They are also part of a structure so orderly and Cartesian that it could only be French. Let me be clear on this point, for it is the only real point I have to make. French sauces are not just a group of randomly assembled essences and emulsions. They come in families, each one of which descends from one basic sauce known appropriately as a *sauce mère* or mother sauce. Once you have made the mother sauce (which is rarely served by itself), you can make all the small or compound sauces (the ones that are served) in a matter of minutes by adding the appropriate special ingredients that make up the particular sauce. For example, once you have prepared a batch of brown sauce (jus de veau, espagnole or demi-glace), all you have to do to produce sauce madère (Madeira sauce) is to add Madeira.

The sauce system is like a group of family trees that evolved over centuries and reached their fullest elaboration in the late nineteenth century. The system was codified by Escoffier after World War I, and it is still the basis for what is called *haute cuisine* or classic cuisine in France today.

Now it is a fact that younger chefs in France have radically "simplified" their menus and no longer cook precisely in the manner of Escoffier. They have dropped the fussy garnishes that used to accompany food served in important restaurants. And, as far as sauces are concerned, they have eliminated or virtually eliminated flour as a thickening agent for the mother sauces. Instead, they reduce their stocks further and use other liaisons: cream, butter, hollandaise and egg yolks, as well as arrowroot.

This amounts to a fundamental change of direction. Its proponents assert that flour muddied the taste of the (now) old-fashioned espagnoles and veloutés. They go on to say that the streamlined nature of modern life demands lighter sauces that do not overwhelm the basic elements of the dish which the sauce accompanies.

These arguments are persuasive up to a point. Flour-bound sauces do tend to be more present as a complex taste and a texture than do sauces based on pure reductions of veal stock. On the other hand, in my opinion it is a slander on the past and an error to dismiss 150 years of professional saucemaking as a muddy, glutinous botch.

For one thing, the antiflour faction never mention that they are saving at least a day's labor every time they do not add roux to stock to make their sauce bases. They don't have to pay someone to stay by the big stock pot skimming for hours at a stretch. True, they do have to use more bones and meat to get their effects, but materials for stock are far less expensive than the salaries of today's restaurant personnel.

Secondly, a well-made demi-glace, which is the highest refinement of brown sauce, does not taste of flour, is not oppressively heavy, and does not overpower the flavors of other foods.

To prove this, I have several times set two sauce boats on the table, one containing a demi-glace based sauce, the other filled with the same sauce prepared from an unthickened "mother." Then, I served double portions of the same dish, one with the old-fashioned sauce, the other with the modern sauce. I have invariably preferred the flour-bound version; so have my guests. We all opted for the more imposing, grand old way.

This is one reason why I have gone to Escoffier's *Guide Culinaire* and other prewar sources, rather than to practicing chefs, for the basic guidelines in preparing this book. The other reason is that the new style is still a-borning; it has not gelled to the point where nonprofessionals should meddle in it. The prewar cuisine, however, is well-defined and accessible to the home cook, who is perfectly capable of turning out impeccable, classic sauces if he/she has a small amount of patience, a large pot, and a fine strainer.

The myth that only chefs with 20 years of experience can make the great sauces well is just that. Certainly, experience helps, but the chef's training is necessary only for running an à la carte restaurant; it does not take a *toque blanche* to make one dish at a time.

There is also a myth, equally false, that sauces are a mystery, an oral tradition passed down from chef to chef. In fact, the great ones, from Taillevent to Carême to Escoffier, have published books and revealed their methods. Escoffier, in particular, was quite candid about quantities.

The real stumbling block with sauces has always been the first step. The quantities of ingredients necessary for *haute cuisine* stocks are large. They have to be, because there is no point in spending two days on an espagnole unless you are going to maximize the effect of your labors and produce a reasonable amount of that liquid gold. And what private person ever needed espagnole by the quart?

No one, of course. And so no one ever tried, except the occasional martyr.

But in this last half of the twentieth century, people cooking at home should try making espagnole and the other basic sauces in quan-

tity because they have freezers. And sauce base freezes very nicely indeed. Put away in small containers, it will stand up well for several
months. Some of my demi-glace has even lasted, without serious loss of
flavor, for a year, although ideally it should be used up before three
months have passed because freezing only slows down normal processes
of biological change.

In any case, experiments I have been conducting in my home for
the past four years prove that classic sauces are within the reach of anyone with normal cooking experience who has enough freezer space to
store two quarts of base.

Furthermore, by tending your stock pot for two or three weekends
a year, you will always have enough base in the house to whip up a
three-star sauce for guests or family, even when you have been out of
the house most of the day. The sauce system was intended for last-
minute cooking. That, after all, is what restaurants are in business to do:
start cooking when the customer orders. And classic sauces made in the
most unremittingly classical manner can almost all be finished while
steak broils or a fish sautés, so long as the chef has his mother sauce
already on hand.

The same thing can easily be true in the home, for, paradoxically,
sauces, which are normally considered the most refined part of cooking,
are also a convenience food at the highest level. This is not my personal
theory; it is the basic principle that made à la carte *haute cuisine* possible. The same economies of time and scale can be achieved by all of us.

This book offers recipes for 111 sauces drawn from the great chefs'
cookbooks of the highest French tradition. They have been scaled down
in size so that most of them will be adequate for six people of average
appetite. Every recipe has been tested with American ingredients and
American equipment. In some instances, where a blender made more
sense than the mortar and pestle of old, or a food mill would suffice
for a tamis, techniques have been modernized. But in every essential
way, the recipes echo the practice of French chefs of the recent past in
their kitchens.

In addition to the sauce recipes, there are also recipes for dishes
to go with them. These "made" dishes should definitely not be thought
of as required companions to the sauces. Indeed, I hope that most
people most of the time will not bother with these purposely ornate
and lavish relics from a happier time. They are meant for the occasional

moment when the urge to cook something difficult or new seizes you. Nearly all of them are faithful re-creations of entrées that used to be served conventionally with the sauces paired with them here.

Those same sauces were, nevertheless, often served with much simpler fare: roasts, steaks, sautéed chicken. I have indicated the general category of food for which each individual sauce was thought appropriate. But these indications are only suggestions. French sauces are far more versatile than the French have led us to believe. As you progress, you will undoubtedly invent new combinations.

You should also feel free to improvise with the sauces themselves. Chefs always have, which is why there are so many recipes for an old chestnut such as sauce grand veneur.

The important thing is to taste and then taste again. All sauces are simple compared to a soufflé. The trick is in balancing those flavor accents that are added at the end and in reducing the sauce to the ideal point. No one can write a recipe prescribing exactly how to achieve perfection in these matters. But who would want to?

Sauces are the last frontier for the cook who has tried everything else. On the frontier, each person must fend for himself, make his own standards. And on this particular frontier, we are about to be especially alone. The day of the luxury restaurant is all but over. The chefs have already started to move in new directions. As a result, if we want to experience some of the most sophisticated tastes ever invented by man, we must make our own sauces. The onus is now on the amateur, but it is a pleasant burden.

A Brief
History
of French
Sauces

In France, there have always been sauces, which is to say that the Franks and the Gauls moistened their food with a flavored liquid. These early sauces, spiced and pungent, sweet and sour, do not, however, qualify as ancestors of what we know today as French sauces. Rather, they—and the sauces served in France until the beginning of the modern period—were a continuation of Roman and Mediterranean practice. Garum, the basic Roman sauce, was made from fermented fish. Typical seasonings were cumin, cardamom, and coriander, as well as honey, perfume, and flower petals.

The Crusades reopened commerce with the East and broadened the palette of exotic spices that French chefs injected into their sauces. The first French cookbook, the celebrated *Viandier* of Taillevent (whose real name was Guillaume Tirel), provides ample proof that the fourteenth century still doted on Oriental tastes. A typical Taillevent sauce for roasts consisted of mustard, red wine, powdered cinnamon, and sugar. Elsewhere, ginger and saffron crop up frequently.

On the other hand, we do detect the beginnings of what we would call sauce in Taillevent's coulis, broths thickened with cream, butter, and egg yolks, which served as the basis of the soups so popular at the time.

Roux was unknown as a thickening agent, and the most common liaison was bread or toast.

The next three hundred years, at least on the evidence of the leading cookbooks that have survived, was a chaos of invention, but few of the extant sauce recipes look like their modern counterparts. For the first half of the fifteenth century, the best indications of the style and substance of the cuisine come from François Rabelais, who catalogues the edible "sacrifices" made by the Gastrolators to their god, Manduco (from the Latin, *manduco,* for glutton). Those two chapters, 59 and 60, in the fourth volume of *Gargantua and Pantagruel* are, of course, satirical, but the endless lists of dishes are comic only in length. They can be assumed to be an accurate rundown of what people ate in the early 1500s. Out of dozens upon dozens of items, only the following came with a sauce: pâtés with hot sauce (*saulce chaulde*) and lampreys with *saulce d'Hippocras* (a sort of early vermouth). Perhaps we should also include among the sauced dishes the pork chops in oignonnade (a purée of onions?), chicken with blanc-mange, mutton shoulder with capers, loin of veal "mustardized" (*sinapisé*) with powdered ginger, and myriad salted fish. In any case, it is clear that the concept of serving food with sauce had not taken hold in Rabelais's time, nor was it usual to build a sauce on a base of stock or coulis.

The impulse for this great leap forward came from Italy. Or at least it can be said with confidence that all commentators agree on the arrival of Catherine de Medici at the court of François I on October 20, 1553, as the dawn of French cuisine as we know it. Only 14, but already betrothed to the future Henry II, Catherine brought with her a retinue of Italian cooks then considered the best in Europe.

No doubt, these fine Italian hands did effect a revolution of refinement in French kitchens, as everyone says. But I confess to puzzlement after reading a contemporary account of the fabled Catherine's favorite foods: coxcombs, cock's kidneys, and artichoke bottoms. At the wedding of a certain Mademoiselle de Martigues, the young princess consumed so many of these delicacies that she almost burst. And, at a dinner in her honor, there was the usual post-medieval assortment of peacocks, swans, cranes, and herons.

Real change, in the sauce repertory, does not crop up in cookbooks until the following century, when the two great themes of French culinary history begin to sound. Virtually all chefs from 1600 on will call both for greater simplicity of service and menu and for greater system in their kitchens. The Cartesian current in French culture now starts to organize gastronomic life. Purity and an easily grasped order will shape the cuisine. These twin principles will most especially determine the course of the development of sauces.

✣❂ LA VARENNE, DE LUNE, AND MASSALIOT: THE SEVENTEENTH CENTURY

It is safe to assume that important cookbooks sum up the traditional practice of the period immediately before their publication. Escoffier, for instance, published the *Guide Culinaire* in 1921, and it sets forth the *haute cuisine* typical of the 20 or 30 years before World War I. In that sense, the influential *Le Nouveau et Parfaict Cuisinier* of Pierre de Lune is a document of the middle 1600s set down and published in the 1660s, when it went into several editions. De Lune is important because he is the last of the ancient masters. He stands with François-Pierre de la Varenne, cook to Henri IV and author of *Le Cuisinier François* (1651), at the threshold of classic cuisine. With La Varenne, we are still presented with the coulis style of saucemaking. Roux is known and discussed in a section on liaisons that can be made in advance. But for his master recipe for brown sauce, La Varenne still uses the old terminology of bouillon (stock) and coulis (sauce base). Moreover, when he adds flour for thickening, he merely throws it into the sauce raw and lets it cook therein. And La Varenne's repertory of sauces includes a poivrade made exclusively from vinegar, salt, onion, orange or lemon peel, and pepper—without any meat stock base—as well as several other sweet-and-sour sauces in the medieval or Renaissance fashion. There is, however, a sauce Robert that sounds almost modern and was served with pork.

De Lune, 10 years later, refers to roux more frequently and prints a recipe for jus de veau that has not been improved on since. On the other hand, he is still ready to throw raw flour into the stock pot, and his list of sauces, as such, is short and premodern. Even the word sauce is used in an antique sense. In a recipe for beef à l'anglaise, he stipulates that the meat should be spit-roasted until half done and then put in a pot with the sauce that has been collected during roasting. Then, he proceeds to enrich these drippings with bouillon, white wine, mushrooms, anchovy, capers, oysters, and "fried flour" (i.e., roux) to make what we would call a sauce.

Dawn finally breaks in 1691 with the appearance of Massaliot's *Le Cuisinier Roïal et Bourgeois.* In it, he declares that "not without some hesitation, the preparation of small sauces is beginning to spread. . . ." By small sauces, he meant what a chef means today: sauces that have been created for a specific use with a big (*grande*) sauce as a base. His sauce brune is thickened with a roux, named as such. And he gives directions for an impressive list of smaller sauces. Their names, aside from Robert and rémoulade, would be unfamiliar to a modern chef, but they are legitimate early examples of compound or little sauces. Nevertheless, Massaliot is still a man of the seventeenth century. He advises thickening a sauce for pheasant with a coulis of partridge, if necessary. His "espagnole" is an antique sauce. It will be another hundred years before the system which he ushers in will mature, in the hands of Carême, into the classic cuisine.

✒ THE EIGHTEENTH CENTURY

This is a puzzling period, because a crucial document is missing. Laguipière, the beloved mentor of Carême, did not leave any record of his undoubtedly important achievements. Without this or any other important cookbook from the last quarter of the century, we cannot more than guess at what occurred during this critical time. The earlier years were undoubtedly an era of consolidation and of expansion. Brillat-Savarin speaks of the eighteenth century as a period of boundless progress. Vincent La Chapelle, author of the most distinguished cookbook of the day (*Le Cuisinier Moderne,* 1733), writes of "new rules" and "new tastes." And the 1700s did see the introduction of beefsteak and potatoes into the French diet as well as the growth of a new gastronomic institution, the restaurant. Members of the royal court invented new dishes, or rather they appropriated the glory for their discovery from helpless chefs. Louis XV's wife, Marie Leczinska, became famous for bouchées à la reine, poulet à la reine, and consommé à la reine, all three invented by La Chapelle, who was also responsible for sirloin filet braised à la royale. Maréchal Villeroy did, evidently, improvise sauce Villeroy himself. Another marshal of France, Mirepoix, invented mirepoix, which subsequently became a standard way of enriching espagnole with vegetable flavors.

The greatest of these noble discoveries, if it in fact occurred, was the world première of mayonnaise, said to have taken place at the table of the Duc de Richelieu, second cousin of the cardinal, after the capture of Port Mahon in 1759.

This is the most disputed of all sauce origins. Some people are persuaded that mahonnaise was indeed transformed into mayonnaise. Others find a more appealing etymology in the old-fashioned word for egg yolk: moyeu. Carême insisted on yet a third alternative: "Some people," he wrote, "say *mayonnaise,* others *mahonnaise,* still others *bayonnaise.* It makes no difference that vulgar cooks should use these words, but I urge that these three terms never be uttered in our great kitchens (where the purists are to be found) and that we should always denominate this sauce with the epithet, *magnonaise.*"

Carême was convinced that his etymology made the most sense: magnonaise came from the verb *"manier,"* to handle or work, which, he argued, was exactly what one did to produce a good mayonnaise. Of course, as the author of the article on this sauce in the *Larousse Gastronomique* points out, this is also true of many other sauces.

If I may further add to the confusion, it seems to me improbable that no one has yet proposed a fourth solution to the problem. Since most sauces are named after places (béarnaise, vénitienne, italienne, africaine), it is logical that mayonnaise refer to one also. Unfortunately, there is no town of Mayonne; however, there is a city in France, at the western edge of Normandy, called Mayenne. Who is to say that mayonnaise did not begin as mayennaise?

At any rate, the sauce repertory did grow during the eighteenth century. The *Dictionnaire Portatif de Cuisine, d'Office et de Distillation* (1767), an anonymous encyclopedia, lists 78 sauces. The stocks and jus are richer than ever. There is an allemande thickened with egg yolks as it would be now. A coulis bound with roux closely resembles a modern brown sauce. Sauce Robert is, as usual by now, in its classic form. And, although something called hollandaise contains beurre manié, bouillon, and anchovy (as well as lemon juice and parsley, but no egg yolk), nevertheless, there is every indication here that the eighteenth-century chefs were converging toward the systematic sauce repertory of the Napoleonic era.

The year 1789 brought the most famous of all political revolutions. It unleashed the forces of modern European civilization. And it set the stage for the imperial career of the first modern cook.

✒️ *CAREME*

Marie-Antoine Carême (1784–1833), who always signed his books Antonin and whose surname incongruously means Lent, the season of restraint at meals, is the towering figure of the entire history of the *grande cuisine* in France. Obsessive, vain, strident, this Napoleon of the kitchen perfected and rationalized 500 years of culinary evolution with as sure a hand as his emperor finished the equally old task of welding France into a governable nation-state.

Anyone who suspects that Carême's reputation is really glory reflected from his masters—Talleyrand, George IV of England, Alexander of Russia, the Baron Rothschild—should search out the man's books, especially *L'Art de la Cuisine Française au Dix-neuvième Siècle.* We will never know how much of what is in those now rare volumes Carême himself invented, or how much he merely borrowed and recast in a new and cogent form. But we can be certain that he defined the official style for French chefs for at least the next century and that he established the supremacy of French cuisine over all other European national styles.

He knew exactly what he was doing—which was to conquer the world with French cooking, just as Napoleon had conquered it with the French army. In *Le Cuisinier Parisien* (1828), in a characteristically imperial mood and in the imperative mode, he wrote:

> Be aware that no foreign sauce is comparable to those of our great modern cuisine. I have been able to experience the difference. I have seen England, Russia, Germany and Italy, and everywhere I have come upon our chefs occupying the top positions in foreign courts.
>
> I will add to *our* espagnole and *our* allemande (I underline the possessive pronouns to emphasize that these sauces are of French origin) sauce suprême, sauce à l'estragon, sauce ravigote, sauce vert-pré, sauce béchamel, sauce financière, sauce Périgueux,

sauce tortue, sauce matelote, sauce au vin de Champagne, sauce à la régence, sauce à la bourguignotte, sauce esturgeon, sauce poivrade, sauce chevreuil, sauce aigre-doux, sauce piquante, sauce salmis, sauce tomate, sauce au levraut liée au sang, sauce parisienne, sauce Robert, sauce raifort, sauce magnonaise, sauce provençale, sauce au beurre d'écrevisses, sauce au homard, sauce aux crevettes, sauce aux huitres, sauce au beurre d'anchois, sauce à la crème, sauce à la pluche, sauce au beurre, called bâtarde, and sauce aux câpres.

We have Frenchified sauce italienne, sauce vénitienne, sauce hollandaise, sauce russe, sauce polonaise, sauce portugaise, sauce milanaise. . . .

The list is grandiose and imperialistic, but, more importantly, it is almost the same list compiled by Escoffier in 1921. And with few differences, the two men were describing identical sauces produced from virtually the same mother sauces.

The crucial point is that Carême articulated for the first time the concept of the mother sauces from which all or almost all other sauces would be made. He enumerated four of them: espagnole, velouté, allemande, and béchamel. Now it is true that, as you will see, these four are really one sauce, but in an actual professional kitchen, it was a matter of practical convenience to prepare batches of all four ahead of time and proceed from there when the need for small sauces arose. As Carême put it: "With these four sauces, we create a great number of small ones whose seasoning is infinitely various."*

This system, he goes on to say, will save time, but he anticipates criticism for his *"nouvelle manière"* and feels it necessary to defend his new method of saucemaking as a shortcut that produces the same results as older methods. "I address myself," says Carême, "to the overwhelming majority of chefs who want to speed up their work while still doing it well."

All of this defensive rhetoric was marshaled in the defense of one technical change. Carême had opted for roux as the universal thickening agent.

* The division of mother sauces in this book is superficially different from Carême's. It did not seem practical for home cooks to produce entirely separate batches of allemande for freezing, since the amount of time necessary for advancing from velouté to allemande is so short. By freezing velouté alone, one preserves a certain versatility at a small sacrifice in efficiency.

As he explains it, up until the end of the reign of Louis XV (who died in 1774), the standard method was to sprinkle raw flour into the stock pot and cook it. Roux gained adherents in the late 1700s, for it could be added after the stock had been refined, and, evidently, there was a net gain in preparation time, because the flour in the roux was already cooked and browned. Evidently also, the time required for skimming away the scum that the roux threw off was less than that used up in refining and finishing a grande sauce thickened with raw flour.

Carême's spirited defense of roux is worth quoting in full, because the contemporary culinary world has once again turned its back on this apparently harmless mixture of butter and flour:

O pitiful writers, how impertinent you are, and foolish! How can you maintain that fresh butter and the purest flour mixed together and cooked with care over the ashes of a slow fire become harmful to health? There are such roux, for great and small sauces, just as there is ink for writers who, senselessly, produce elementary texts on the various trades without possessing clear ideas of their subject; they do not know that our roux, prepared according to the principles enunciated above, have a nutty taste that is pleasing even to the most innocent palate; that these roux, once blended and dissolved in a sauce, first bind the sauce and then are separated from it by the boiling action to which we subject the sauce in order to degrease it; that the pot containing the thickened sauce is always placed at the edge of the stove so that the scum and the butter are thrown off on the side of the pot away from where it is boiling; that the butter which we then remove, and which is used again to make roux, has not undergone the slightest alteration, and that it has the same color as when it was first mixed with flour to obtain roux.

Now, I ask these makers of silly books, in what way can this process of mixing butter and flour become corrosive and incendiary? I repeat, if these vain compilers had the slightest degree of good sense, they would know that the clarification of *grandes sauces* relieves them entirely of every trace of roux, but that roux is fundamentally necessary to bind and give body to them, that without this procedure of cooking the roux, the flour and butter would combine imperfectly; that, as a result, the sauces would be imperfectly bound and would turn into simple essences during reduction, and that, thus, they would be neither smooth (*veloutées*) nor succulent. But what does this matter to these ignorant men? As long as they can babble and publish their dull screeds, they don't care at all if they cheapen a man's trade. However, sooner or later, a well-informed professional may come along, who will unmask these vile mountebanks and, revenging Science, make them disappear from the world's stage.

Enough said, except that this debate has now shifted to a new ground. The anti-roux faction, once again ascendant, asserts that it can obtain lighter, finer results without using flour at all, whether mixed with butter or added raw. Carême's response to this would undoubtedly be that these exquisite reductions are only essences and lack the body and velvet consistency which he described with the untranslatable adjective velouté.

AFTER CAREME

For more than a century, chefs in France followed the example of Carême. Indeed, during the entire remainder of the nineteenth century and, roughly speaking, the first half of the twentieth, the great names of the culinary profession occupied themselves principally with refining and streamlining his work. The master's *pièces montées*, extravaganzas of (sometimes) edible architecture, were the first of his legacies to be abandoned. His disciple, Jules Gouffé, lopped off scores of recipes from the thousands in the original Carême corpus and added more explicit, quantified directions for the dishes he retained. Prosper Montagné, Philéas Gilbert, and Escoffier each contributed to the slimming of Carême, although today, when almost nothing as formal as their cuisine remains, it is difficult to think of the authors of the *Guide Culinaire* and the *Larousse Gastronomique* as simplifiers. But such they were, while at the same time they absorbed into their canon of recipes the new dishes and sauces created during their lifetimes. Béarnaise and Véron were both nineteenth-century creations. The former was made for the first time at the Pavillon Henri IV at Saint-Germain-en-Laye outside Paris and was named for the native province of the long-dead king. Sauce Véron commemorates the Dr. Véron who managed the Opéra-Comique and used the profits to pay for the Lucullan dinners prepared by his legendary housekeeper Sophie every day of the week for 30 favored guests.

Although talented chefs continued to cook creatively in the grand tradition of Carême—indeed, many are still hard at work—by the end of World War I, *haute cuisine* had calcified. Escoffier gave it its final expression in his magisterial *Guide Culinaire*. And, at almost the same moment that this last of the nineteenth-century *haute cuisine* chef's manuals appeared, in the 1920s, the greatest of all gastronomic journalists, Curnonsky (born Maurice-Edmond Sailland), turned public attention away from the outmoded world of *haute cuisine* and toward the still vigorous but half-forgotten traditions of French regional cooking.

Since then, the influence of Curnonsky—and of the wide number of readers whom he taught to admire *la cuisine des femmes*—encouraged a new generation of twentieth-century chefs to open restaurants specializing in regional dishes. A leader of this new school of cooks, Alexandre Dumaine, combined the elegance and complication of classic cooking with the basic splendor of the dishes of Burgundy, the setting of his renowned restaurant at Saulieu. Not far from there, at Vienne near Lyons, the equally illustrious Fernand Point went his own way, which was to marshal all the culinary science of the past in order to focus the mind and palate on a single main ingredient or a central gastronomic idea. Point believed Curnonsky's dictum that food should "taste of what it is." And he was famous for his fanatic attention to such apparently simple tasks as frying an egg. Although he was not above preparing a peasant dish of corn flour simmered in chicken stock and finished with cream, more characteristically he devoted himself to the glorification of the products of his region. The Point touch was pure and dramatic, unencumbered by dominating sauces and distracting side dishes. His food was not simple; he strove, instead, for a simple effect. The flair of Point and his disciples is not, however, something American amateurs can easily try to match. We lack both the extraordinary raw materials and the professional training needed to coordinate his "simple" food ideas. But we can operate, within certain judicious limitations, after the manner of Escoffier and Carême. The techniques for classic saucemaking are well-established and straightforward. The classic sauces themselves open up a grand storehouse of abandoned dishes and tastes that are particularly appropriate to our time and place. While restaurants have had to give them up for economic reasons, classic sauces are entirely feasible in a private home, and they enhance, but do not overwhelm, the products of agribusiness if they are properly made and flavored, and especially if they are enriched with the cooking liquid of the food they will join.

How to Use This Book

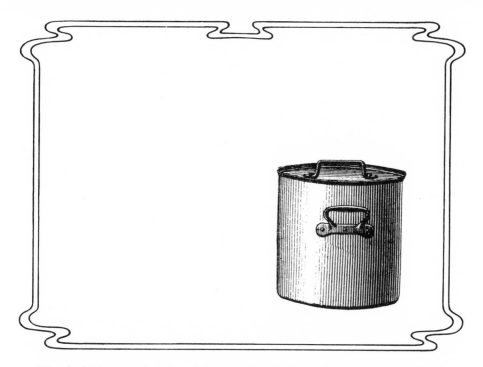

You hold in your hands a labor-saving device. I know this sounds like a preposterous claim for a cookbook whose first recipe requires two days to complete. But it is so. Here is why.

Once you have simmered and strained and skimmed your demi-glace or velouté to perfection, you not only have a very fine sauce base—better than or as good as anything you will find used in the best French restaurants—you also have money in the bank. That is to say, you have already done most of the work for several dinners, weeks ahead of time.

For example, on a certain rainy fall weekend when you would otherwise putter about the house anyway, patching plaster, watching television, darning socks, instead you start the day by browning some bones and meat and vegetables, set them simmering in water, and then you do whatever you like all Saturday. Twelve hours later, you will have a peerless brown stock (or in much less time you will have a white stock or a fish velouté).

On Sunday, it is still raining. You make a roux after breakfast, and a mirepoix (more browned vegetables), remove the layer of fat that has solidified on top of your stock, and proceed to the ultimate refinement of your mother sauce. Mostly this means a lot of skimming. As it reduces—cooks down—the sauce will throw off scum. The more you remove, the finer the sauce in the end. And so you establish yourself with a copy of the Bible or *Fanny Hill,* or whatever you like to read on Sunday, on a comfortable chair in the vicinity of the stove. Every 15 minutes or so, you make a careful sweep across the surface of your ever-richening sauce with your trusty skimmer. Then back to Bathsheba or the misadventures of Ms. Hill.

Later in the day, you have got your mother sauce tucked away in the freezer. A little fuss, a little muss, but for the next 20 dinner parties you will be known as the cool of the evening. No all-day, sweat-raising feats of culinary self-sacrifice for you. You can produce *haute cuisine* à l'Escoffier in minutes.

On the morning of your intimate dinner, you make your most critical move: You extract a 1-cup container of demi-glace from your freezer and put it out to defrost. For the rest of the day, you go about your business. On the way home, you pick up six artichokes, six pork chops, cheese, fruit, and whatever staples you may need. The artichokes blanch while you shower. They will be served cold with your favorite vinaigrette, mixed in half a minute. Set the table and relax. During the cocktail hour, slip away for a few minutes, chop and sauté an onion, then cook the onion in ⅔ cup of white wine until most of the liquid has boiled away, pour in the demi-glace and let the sauce simmer for a few minutes. Season with a little sugar and some mustard. Voilà, sauce Robert, a standard pork sauce dating from at least the seventeenth century. Keep it hot in a bain-marie (a pan of simmering water) and put the pork chops under the broiler. Serve the artichokes. Dinner is ready.

Admittedly, not all sauces can be thrown together quite so quickly. But, actually, most of them can, so long as you have the mother sauce done in advance. And since almost all sauces will go well with foods that cook quickly—steaks and chops, roasts and cuts that can be sautéed or deep-fried—your single rainy weekend by the stove has set you up as a grand party-giver who uses only the most elegant methods but spends all day at the office, the track, or wherever you like to spend the day.

The example I have given presupposes that you have started out with the most elaborate and time-consuming sauce base—demi-glace. The veloutés are significantly quicker, especially fish velouté. And, of course, many classic sauces—béarnaise, hollandaise, and their variations—require no advance preparation.

On the other hand, if you are in the mood for an athletic afternoon in the kitchen, *haute cuisine* offers you endless hours of knife-flashing diversion. In other words, if you want to make a complicated dish to go with your sauce, the sky is the limit.

I have combed the older cookbooks and chefs' memoranda looking for dishes that were and are appropriate for these sauces. There is at least one such recipe printed after almost every sauce recipe. Almost all the dishes were traditionally combined with the sauces they are paired with here. Every attempt has been made to keep all these recipes authentic.

Still, this is 1975 and some changes are unavoidable. Culinary historians will notice that I have sometimes eliminated the garniture— the side dishes or decoration—once called for and now, since tastes have altered and kitchen staffs have gone the way of all flesh, no longer practical or desirable. Anyone who feels stung by these omissions, which are not frequent, may of course gussy up his platter with artichoke bottoms, fluted mushrooms, and pastry swans. Most people will find plenty of these traditional curlicues already present in the text as it is.

At any rate, nothing in these pages should be regarded as sacrosanct. All recipes are only guideposts, and this is most definitely true of sauce recipes, for which there has never been and will never be agreement among professionals. Unfortunately, however, gastronomy seems to inspire people with self-righteous certainty, and I fully expect to receive a reasonable facsimile of the following letter:

Sir:

How dare you presume to print a recipe for Sauce Grand Veneur without truffle essence. Yours is no Sauce Grand Veneur. It is nothing but partridge soup, a mean swill unfit to serve even with the feet of the noble stag.

Signed Outraged

My reply will go something like this:

I assume you have not tried making "my" sauce grand veneur (which is not mine, to be fair, but a synthesis of recipes printed in standard French sources), and I urge you to do so. Your passion for truffle essence is understandable; I am sure even my poor "swill" of a game sauce will be improved by that noble liquor.

Nevertheless, Sir, I feel compelled to remind you that the

definitions of the classic sauces have always been loose. The greatest chefs have always varied in their practice, and the essential meaning of sauce names cannot usefully be specified further than a few simple indications. For sauce Robert, which is better documented over a longer period than any other sauce still in common use, we can say little more than that it consists of a brown base seasoned more or less highly with onion, a white wine reduction, and other flavorings. To go further is to mistake the nature of the subject. What matters is the ultimate taste. I would invite you next Thursday when we will be serving the sauce you find so dubious (with a saddle of venison shot by my nephew and now marinating with fresh juniper berries), but my wife takes the position that she will suffer fools gladly by day, but not at dinner.

Yr. humble servant, etc.

The above notwithstanding, I have hewed as closely as possible to actual recipes published by distinguished French authorities, conforming them to American measurements and conditions but not to some new standard invented by me.

"Very well," you may ask, "but what will all this cost?"

Like all food in this period of chronic shortages and economic mismanagement, these recipes will not be cheap. But they are not more expensive than other dishes you would serve to guests. Or, at least, the margin of increase in expense added by the sauce is negligible.

To take the most extravagant example—demi-glace—it may at first glance strike you as outrageous to spend $30 in raw materials to produce 5 quarts of sauce base. Since, however, that quantity will account for 20 dinners (5 quarts equals 20 cups and most of the recipes use 1 cup of base) for 6 people, the cost per serving works out to 25 cents per guest. Let's assume the worst, that prices go up 50% between the time I write this and the day you go to the butcher shop with your grandiose order for "soup bones." We are now up to $37\frac{1}{2}$ cents per guest. And, for good measure, let's round off to a total of 50 cents per person, to account for additional ingredients used to complete the sauce: shallots, wine, etc.

All these estimates exaggerate the average cost of serving classic sauces, but they still add only $3 to the total bill for dinner. At the moment, it would be more realistic to say that you will really be spending less than $2 extra overall, which is less than it costs to have two drinks in a bar.

It is certainly not the case either that these sauces have to be served only with the most expensive cuts of meat. I have purposely included recipes for everything from eggs to kidneys in order to show the versatility of French sauces. Indeed, one of the virtues of sauces is that they dress up dishes that we might otherwise disdain for their plainness.

ஜ UTENSILS

You will probably have to buy a large pot, as well as a few other special utensils.

» There is no way to make stock in quantity without a large stock pot. I recommend that you invest in a professional quality, heavy-gauge aluminum pot that will hold 35–40 quarts. If you can get one with a spigot, that will help you a great deal, since a fully loaded 40-quart pot is impossible to lift. Without a spigot, you will have to bail out your stock with a saucepan. This is not as difficult as it sounds, but it can be messy.

Buy your stock pot from a restaurant supply outlet. Conventional gourmet equipment stores usually offer an inadequate selection of large pots and overcharge for them. I was able to purchase an 80-quart pot with lid for $35 from a restaurant supply shop in 1973.

You will also need a second large pot into which you can pour your stock or base after it is finished and needs a clean place to cool. Probably you have an old lobster pot, which would be ideal. Otherwise, any 20-quart pot (or a collection of smaller ones) will do.

» A skimmer is a long-handled tool with a perforated disk on the end. You can also skim with a slotted spoon, but a skimmer is faster and more efficient.

» A chinois is a cone-shaped strainer with a very fine metal mesh. It is a marvelous tool with an infinity of uses. For instance, it will transform partly curdled custards into velvet. Also, it is ideal for straining sauce base and stock. And you cannot make a fine sauce without it, unless you like to squeeze gallons of hot liquid through muslin.

To go with your chinois, get something that will agitate the sauce while it strains slowly through the mesh. I use a wooden device sold for frothing hot chocolate. It has a fluted knob at the end that fits almost all the way to the bottom of the chinois. By twirling and plunging with this gadget, you speed up the straining.

» If you do not already have one, a heavy enameled or stainless-steel saucepan is *de rigueur* for sauces with wine in them. Aluminum reacts with the wine.

» Finally, buy enough 1- or 2-cup freezer containers to accommodate 20 cups of mother sauce. The small size permits rapid defrosting. (If you refreeze a defrosted stock or base, you must boil it first to prevent spoilage.)

I do not recommend ordering large pots by mail because of the expense for shipping, but smaller items are available from the following:

The Bridge Company
212 East 52 Street
New York, N.Y. 10022

Williams-Sonoma
576 Sutter Street
San Francisco, Calif. 94102

INGREDIENTS FOR SUCCESS

The only common ingredient in these recipes not universally available in big-city markets in this country is shallots. Do not fret about shallots. It is nice to have them, but even the ones that do appear in sophisticated markets are an inferior variety and expensive. They do, however, keep for long periods in the refrigerator, and one box goes a long way. If you can't find them, substitute scallions, white part only.

Use local fish whenever possible. It will be fresher. Catfish caught today will always taste better than fancy Dover sole frozen last week (or month?), and even so-called "fresh" fish shipped great distances in ice is no bargain.

Seek out the largest fishmonger in your town (largest in terms of business volume, not girth). He will be in a much better position to save scraps for you if he knows who you are and if you call him a day in advance. My fish man, a retailer near the Fulton Fish Market in New York, did a double take the first time I came in to order 15 pounds of flounder trimmings for stock. "Are you a mink breeder?" he asked.

Butchers need advance notice, too, for outsize orders of veal shank and beef shin. Always try to get the bones splintered in the store. Serious butchers feel guilty charging you for bones and you should use this as a moral wedge. At the very least, insist that bones be cut into 3-inch sections.

MATTERS OF TECHNIQUE

Unusual technical maneuvers involved in these recipes are explained in the text. I am assuming, however, that no one will use this book who does not have some background in French cooking. I have not, therefore, gone into detail about basic processes, such as sautéing, except where there seemed a special opportunity for confusion. Should you be in doubt about a technical term—and I have used very few—consult the standard explanations in *Mastering the Art of French Cooking,* Julia Child, et al., Knopf: New York, 1961.

Some special problems do arise in saucemaking simply because of the quantity of raw materials you start with. It may be helpful to remember that liquids come to a boil faster when the pot is covered. Four gallons of water plus 30 pounds of solids can take over half an hour to reach 212 degrees. It helps to set the pot over as many burners as it will straddle.

Let stock cool uncovered. Covered stock will spoil as it cools.

"Reduce" means to boil a liquid down, to condense it. Most reduction occurs over high heat at a full boil. If the liquid becomes too dense and risks burning, transfer it to a smaller pot and continue to reduce to the desired volume, stirring.

The exception to this principle is with sauces containing milk or cream. Regulate the heat so that the liquid simmers. A full boil will often cause the sauce to foam up and overflow the pot.

During reduction, if you think there is a chance of burning, stir with a wooden spoon, or best of all, use a chef's spatula, which is a flat wooden blade. It will clean the bottom of the pot with each sweep. A wire whisk works almost as well.

When a recipe directs you to reduce by half or by two-thirds, this is meant as a rough indication of how far to go, not as a sacred part of a chemical formula. Trust your instincts and your eyes. If you want to do a rough measurement, hold a chopstick or the handle of a wooden spoon straight up in the sauce before reduction begins. Mark the point where the surface of the sauce hits the wood. Then calculate the halfway point (or two-thirds down the chopstick or wherever) and gauge the progress of the reduction from time to time by dipping the graduated chopstick into the sauce.

You will also want to have some way of knowing what volume of liquid you have in a large, ungraduated stock pot. When there are solid ingredients in the pot as well, there is no way of measuring the liquid (short of pouring it out), but you can mark the water level on the inside of the pot with a pencil before you start to simmer the stock so that you will know how much more water to put in later.

When only liquid is involved, you can calculate the volume in a cylindrical pot during reduction as follows. Take a clean wooden yardstick and measure the diameter of the pot (the greatest distance from interior wall to interior wall) holding the yardstick level across the top of the pot. Half the diameter is the radius. Note that down. Now measure the height of the liquid in the pot. Finally, get out a pad of paper and use the following formula:

$$\frac{3.14 \times \text{radius}^2 \times \text{height}}{57.75} = \text{liquid volume in quarts}$$

In other words, if your pot is 8 inches across and has 9 inches of stock in it, you have 7.8 quarts ($3.14 \times 4 \times 4 \times 9$ divided by 57.75, which is the number of cubic inches in a quart). Since stock-pot bottoms are not usually perfectly flat, this elaborate figuring never produces a totally accurate result. Remember, though, that if you overreduce, you can always put water back in.

And you can also save yourself some long division by another method of measurement. If the recipe says that you should reduce the stock to 5 quarts, simply pour 5 quarts of water into the empty pot before you start. Mark off the depth of the liquid on a dowel or just continue using the yardstick as a dipstick during reduction. If 5 quarts of water is 6 inches deep in your pot, 5 quarts of stock will be also. Remember to pour off the water used for measurement before you pour in the stock.

❧ SHORTCUTS

I want to say "There aren't any," but centuries of corner-cutting by professionals have proved that there are many ways to skin an espagnole. The most legitimate is to substitute extra bones for the meat in the stock recipes. In its official textbook, the French national hotel school system prints bones-only stock recipes. The resulting taste is less rich, but not at all to be spurned. The financial saving is obvious. And it is rather late in the game to start worrying about cutting back on meat in stocks. Escoffier himself radically reduced the ingredients in stocks. Compared to the vast number of massacred game birds and cattle that used to give their juices to the sauces of his predecessors, his quantities were unconscionably skimpy. Today, we think his list of stock ingredients is sumptuous.

Other shortcuts will endanger the purity and magnificence of your product. But if the task of browning 30 pounds of meat, bone, and vegetable daunts you utterly, there is nothing to stop you from halving (or quartering) the master recipe for brown stock. The result will be the same. There will simply be less of it—and you will have invested almost as much time as if you had made the full amount. The important thing with sauces, as with everything else, is to please yourself.

Brown Sauces

Brown
Sauces

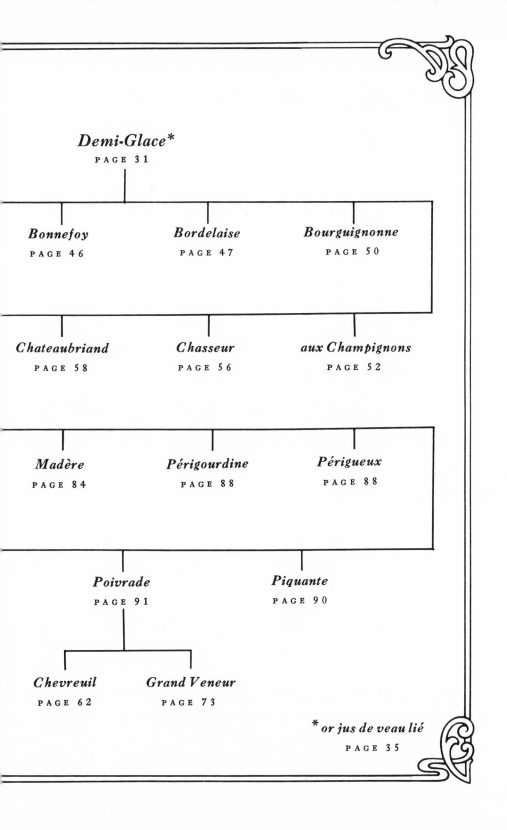

Demi-Glace*

PAGE 31

Bonnefoy

PAGE 46

Bordelaise

PAGE 47

Bourguignonne

PAGE 50

Chateaubriand

PAGE 58

Chasseur

PAGE 56

aux Champignons

PAGE 52

Madère

PAGE 84

Périgourdine

PAGE 88

Périgueux

PAGE 88

Poivrade

PAGE 91

Piquante

PAGE 90

Chevreuil

PAGE 62

Grand Veneur

PAGE 73

* *or jus de veau lié*

PAGE 35

✎ DEMI-GLACE, JUS DE VEAU, AND GLACE DE VIANDE

Sauces made from demi-glace have a body, a monumental size to them, which cannot be produced with even the finest jus de veau lié. And although in this book the recipes for small brown sauces call in every case for *either* demi-glace or jus de veau, you ought, at least once in your cooking life, to follow the longer process for demi-glace through to its magnificent finish.

At the risk of scaring people off demi-glace altogether, but in order to give a straightforward forecast of what is involved, I have printed the entire marathon as one continuous operation, instead of dividing it up into deceptively separate packages (stock, espagnole, roux, and demi-glace) as most classic sources do.

Look closely at the text, and you will see that it takes time but does not require the precision of many cooking jobs at which you are already adept. Moreover, if you simply will not give up the full amount of time for the whole master recipe, stop after you have reached the espagnole stage. You will end up with a very nice mother sauce, and you will have twice as much, in volume, as you would if you pressed on to the end. Espagnole can be used interchangeably with demi-glace and jus de veau in the small sauce recipes.

✎ *GLACE DE VIANDE*

You may want to reserve 1 quart of your stock for making glace de viande (meat glaze). Glace de viande is simply stock reduced by three-quarters (in this case, to 1 cup) or until it turns syrupy and coats the back of a metal spoon. An intense source of flavor, it is called for in several of the recipes that follow. The reduction goes so far that there is some risk of burning the stock, and you should be prepared to keep transferring it to ever-smaller saucepans. Pour the completed glace de viande into a wide-mouthed jar, cool uncovered, then seal and refrigerate. It will solidify and keep almost indefinitely. If molding occurs, run hot water into the jar and wash it away. The glace de viande will still be wholesome underneath.

Whether you are making stock, jus de veau, espagnole, or glace de viande, do not be tempted to add salt. Salt has been intentionally omitted from these recipes. It will be added to the small sauces. Mother sauces have to be reduced too significantly; salting them is dangerous, because the salt does not disappear during reduction. It stays there and its taste intensifies in direct proportion to the degree of reduction. Indeed, one of the principal advantages of homemade over commercial stocks is that they can be severely reduced without turning to brine.

❧ DEMI-GLACE

(HALF-GLAZE)

13 pounds beef shin, with bones
    cut into 3-inch pieces   *or see step 1*
13 pounds veal shank, with bones *for alternative*
    cut into 3-inch pieces
8 tablespoons (1 stick) butter
2 pounds carrots, peeled and sliced in rounds
10 medium onions, peeled and sliced
1½ pounds pork rind, cut into 3-inch squares
1 fresh pig's foot (optional), split
1 bunch parsley
1 tablespoon plus 1 teaspoon fresh or 1¼ teaspoons dried thyme
14 bay leaves
1 clove garlic, finely chopped
1 pound unsalted butter
3¾ cups sifted all-purpose flour
¼ pound salt pork, diced
2 recipes Sauce Tomate (page 212), or 4 pounds whole canned
    Italian tomatoes, drained, seeded, and finely chopped
1 cup Madeira

1. Cut meat away from the beef and veal bones. (A perfectly acceptable sauce can be made entirely from the equivalent weight of beef and veal bones, without meat.) Slice meat into 2-inch cubes. Your butcher may be willing to separate the meat from the bones. He may, if

you are on excellent terms, be willing to split the bones and splinter them with a cleaver. Otherwise you may want to consider carefully whether to splinter them yourself (see directions on page 37). Splintered bones offer a far greater surface area to be browned (which will improve the color of the sauce), and they will yield up their gelatin more efficiently. But unsplit bones will still make an admirable stock.

2. Preheat the oven to 400 degrees.

3. Brown bones in a roasting pan, in batches. Do not use more than one level of the oven at a time. Roast the bones until they have turned a deep caramel color, turning them over once. Keep looking in the oven to make sure they are not burning.

4. While the bones are browning, set a 35- to 40-quart stock pot over as many burners as it will straddle (two 20-quart pots will work as well so long as you divide all quantities in the succeeding steps evenly between the two pots), fill it with 16 quarts (4 gallons or 64 cups) of cold water, cover, and bring to a full, rolling boil. This may take as long as 45 minutes.

5. While you are browning the bones and waiting for the water to boil, melt the 8 tablespoons of butter in a large skillet and sauté $1\frac{1}{2}$ pounds of the carrot rounds and 8 of the sliced onions together until the onions are transparent. If the stock pot is covering all of your burners, push it off of one of them so that you can do this and the next step. Replace it, if it hasn't boiled by then.

6. Blanch the pork rind in enough simmering, unsalted water to cover, for 5 minutes. Drain and reserve.

7. When the water boils, move the pot so that it covers only one or, at most, two burners. Add the browned bones (discarding any burned pieces, which will contribute nothing except a burned taste), the sautéed carrot rounds and onion slices, the blanched pork rind, the split pig's foot (if used), the parsley, 1 tablespoon of the fresh or 1 teaspoon of the dried thyme, 12 of the bay leaves, and the garlic.

8. Return to the boil, reduce heat and simmer for 12 to 15 hours, half covered. This can be done overnight, but experience suggests that if you begin the slow simmering in the morning, that leaves ample waking time for occasional supervision of the liquid level, which can more conveniently be topped up with boiling water little by little rather than all at once the next morning. Also, if you simmer by day, you will then have the late night and early morning for cooling the stock, a lengthy but automatic process that does not require your presence.

9. While the stock simmers, brown the meat cubes on all sides in a heavy pan. As with the bones, successful browning is essential to the color of the sauce. Rendered fat from the meat cubes themselves eliminates the necessity for oil, except perhaps to get the first batch going. Do not crowd the pan. High heat is essential to browning. The cubes should stick to the surface of the pan and turn a caramel color before you turn them. A cube has six sides, and all of them are equal in importance. Reserve the browned meat in a large bowl.

10. Two hours before the bones have finished simmering, add the browned meat cubes to the stock. Bring to a full boil again, skim, reduce heat and simmer for the remaining time, half covered. Note the new water level. It should be maintained with additions of boiling water as before.

11. Clarify the unsalted butter. Cut it into chunks, melt it in a saucepan, and then let stand in an untrafficked place for 30 minutes, while the white milk solids settle out. Some milk solids will float to the surface. Skim them away and discard them. Spoon the clarified butter into a clean container (or directly into a clean skillet), leaving all solid debris on the bottom of the saucepan. You will probably have slightly more clarified butter than the 22 tablespoons you need for the roux for this recipe. Refrigerate the excess. The surplus is intentional, so that the most profligate clarifier will end up with the necessary minimum.

12. Make a brown roux. Heat the 22 tablespoons of clarified butter (1 cup plus 6 tablespoons), in a *heavy* skillet. Remove the skillet from heat and whisk in all the flour as quickly as you can, to make a homogeneous, buttery paste. Cook the roux over medium-low heat, stirring occasionally, until it begins to turn a nut brown. During the final stages of this slow, possibly hour-long process, you must stir the roux frequently to prevent burning. Lower heat so that you can control the coloration. Good brown roux will look almost the same color as chocolate. Discard any burned particles. They will transmit their taste to the sauce. Also, burned roux will not thicken the sauce.

13. Remove finished roux from the skillet immediately, cool, and reserve in the refrigerator.

14. When the stock has finished simmering, remove as many solid ingredients as you can with a skimmer. Discard everything but the meat cubes, which can be eaten as they are, hot from the pot, or ground up for croquettes and patties.

15. Strain the stock through a chinois. Ladle out a quart at a time

with a saucepan or dipper. The stock will cool faster if strained into several smaller pots or bowls; you'll need a total capacity of about 15 quarts. Do *not* cover these pots until the stock has cooled or it will curdle.

16. Early the next morning, refrigerate the stock, so that the fat that has risen to the top will solidify for easy removal. Fat-free stock can be frozen or it can be kept in the refrigerator, so long as you reboil it every 2 or 3 days. You can also remove fat from liquid, room-temperature stock with a flat spoon and soak up the last traces by running sheets of paper toweling over the surface. You will have at least one more chance to remove fat, so don't be compulsive about trapping every last globule at this point. You should, however, get rid of virtually all of it.

17. On the day you choose to press on to the espagnole stage, put 7 quarts of the fat-free stock into a clean stock pot (of at least 20 quarts) over high heat.

18. While the stock heats up, make a mirepoix. Heat the salt pork in a heavy enameled or cast-iron skillet (tinned copper surfaces will bubble under the ensuing heat), discard pork cubes as they brown, and use the rendered fat to sauté the remaining carrots and onions until the onions are transparent. Drain well.

19. Just before the stock begins to simmer, pour a quart or so of it over the roux in a saucepan. Whisk until the roux has dissolved. Use more stock, if necessary. Then pour the mixture back into the stock pot and whisk until thoroughly blended with the stock. Bring to a full boil, lower heat and simmer slowly, uncovered.

20. Add the mirepoix as well as the remaining thyme and bay leaves.

21. Skim every 10 minutes for 1 hour. Strain through a chinois, pressing lightly on the vegetables to extract juices. Wash out the stock pot.

22. Return the strained, thickened stock to the stock pot. Add 2 more quarts of unthickened, fat-free stock. Bring to a boil once more. Reduce heat and simmer for 2 more hours, skimming regularly.

23. Stir in the tomato sauce or tomatoes and continue to simmer and skim for another hour. The scum will have changed to red from the tomatoes. The sauce should already be of an impressive quality, rich and substantial, brown and aromatic.

24. Strain through a chinois lined with muslin or a clean dish towel into a clean pot that will hold 8 quarts or more. If the sauce has not already reduced to 5 quarts, do so over high heat, skimming frequently. You now have espagnole.

25. To make demi-glace, add the remaining fat-free, unthickened stock to the espagnole. Boil, reduce heat and simmer until the liquid reduces to slightly less than 5 quarts. Skim throughout the reduction.

26. Strain through a chinois lined with muslin or a clean dish towel into a clean pot. Stir in the Madeira. Let cool, uncovered, to room temperature. There should not be any fat risen to the surface, but if there is, remove it with great scruple. Pour the demi-glace into small (1- or 2-cup) containers, cover, and freeze.

MAKES 5 QUARTS (20 CUPS)

JUS DE VEAU LIE
(THICKENED VEAL STOCK)

18 pounds veal bones, cut into 3-inch sections
2 pounds carrots, peeled and sliced in rounds
1 pound onions, peeled and sliced
16 cloves garlic, peeled
½ cup tomato paste
8 bay leaves
16 parsley stems
8 sprigs fresh or 2 teaspoons dried thyme
2 pounds mushrooms, wiped clean and roughly chopped
1½ teaspoons fresh or ½ teaspoon dried chervil
1½ teaspoons fresh or ½ teaspoon dried tarragon
1 cup Madeira
2 tablespoons plus 2 teaspoons arrowroot

1. Splinter bones with a cleaver (see page 37). This is an optional procedure.

2. Preheat oven to 400 degrees.

3. Brown the bones in batches in a roasting pan in the oven, turning once. Do not use more than one level of the oven at a time. While the bones are coloring to a caramel shade, set your large stock pot over as many burners as it will straddle. Cover the bottom of the empty pot with carrots, onions, garlic, tomato paste, bay leaves, parsley stems, and thyme. Then add the browned bones, batch by batch, until they are all in the pot.

4. Cover pot, without adding water, and apply high heat for 10 minutes to force the vegetables and bones to "sweat" (French, *suer*), or release their juices.

5. Pour a cup of water into the pot. Continue cooking over high heat until the liquid has reduced to a brown glaze at the bottom. This will take a few minutes, but it is crucial to a flavorful, well-colored *jus*. Repeat this process (known as *pinçage* or pinching) twice more. In order to tell when a glaze has formed, you ought to shift the solid ingredients away from one side of the pot with a long-handled wooden spoon to make a sort of peephole.

6. Now add 10 quarts of cold water and bring to a full boil. Skim carefully, reduce heat and simmer, uncovered, for 6 hours. Unless the water level falls dramatically (which should not happen under normal circumstances), do not add extra water, as the stock is meant to reduce to 8 quarts during the 6 hours of simmering.

7. Remove all solid ingredients with a skimmer and discard. Strain stock through a chinois into a clean pot or pots, cool to room temperature, uncovered, and refrigerate.

8. When the stock has chilled thoroughly, remove the layer of fat that has solidified at the surface. This fat-free stock can be kept in the refrigerator so long as it is reboiled every 2 to 3 days.

9. To complete the jus de veau, add mushrooms, chervil, and tarragon leaves to the strained, fat-free stock and bring to a boil. You will now reduce the stock to 2 quarts of liquid. Since the mushrooms make it difficult to estimate the volume of liquid in the pot, remove them with a skimmer when the reduction looks about half done. Squeeze the mushrooms to make them release the liquid they have absorbed. Now finish the reduction. (Actually, it is probably shrewd to leave an extra cup or so of liquid, to account for waste, spillage, and the margin of error produced by most systems of measurement used during reduction.)

10. Strain through a chinois lined with muslin or a clean dish towel into 1- or 2-cup freezer containers, cool, uncovered, and remove fat once more after refrigeration, if necessary. Freeze.

11. Before using, defrost the required amount of *jus*. Then, in the

proportion of 2 tablespoons Madeira and 1 teaspoon arrowroot per cup of *jus,* dissolve arrowroot in Madeira and stir the mixture into the *jus.* Boil for 1 minute.

MAKES 2 QUARTS

ON SPLITTING BONES

This is exhausting and even dangerous work until you get the hang of it. Bone chips fly here and there. Therefore, it is a good idea to protect your kitchen by spreading newspaper everywhere around you and even taping it to nearby walls. Put on goggles to protect your eyes. Do your pounding on an expendable old cutting board, and buy the heaviest cleaver you can find. The weight of the cleaver does the work.

Stand the bone on end (or hold it on end if it is long and you are confident of your aim). Bring the cleaver down hard so that it cuts into the bone and sticks there. Then raise cleaver and the attached bone and smash the bone against the board, again and again, until the bone splits. Then splinter the halves of the bone into smaller pieces. Don't bother to splinter joints. It can be done but it isn't worth the trouble.

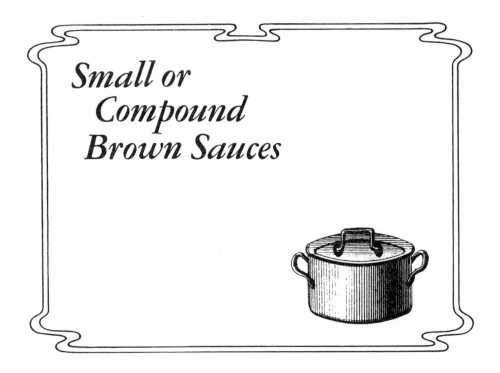

Small or Compound Brown Sauces

SAUCE AFRICAINE

An ultra-refined version of spicy African/Creole flavors, this sauce supports the claim of Roger Fessaguet of The Caravelle restaurant in New York that the *grande cuisine* of France has absorbed food ideas from all over the world. The basic method is, however, the same as in most of the other small brown sauces. Special flavorings are cooked, reduced in wine, and combined with the mother sauce.

Serve with steaks, chops, and chicken.

1 tablespoon oil
1 medium onion, finely chopped
1 medium tomato, peeled, seeded, and finely chopped (see Note)
1 green bell pepper, peeled, seeded, and finely chopped (see Note)
Salt
Paprika
1 small clove garlic, put through a garlic press
3 parsley stems tied in a bouquet with 1 bay leaf, 1 sprig fresh basil, and 1 sprig fresh thyme (or else dust the parsley bouquet with dried basil and thyme)

½ cup dry white wine
1 cup demi-glace or thickened jus de veau (page 31 or 35)

1. Heat the oil in a skillet and sauté onion in it until softened.

2. Add tomato, green pepper, salt, paprika, garlic, parsley, bay leaf, basil, and thyme. Sauté for about 10 minutes.

3. Add white wine and reduce over high heat for 2 to 3 minutes.

4. Add demi-glace or jus de veau. Bring to a boil, reduce heat and simmer for 15 minutes. Remove parsley bouquet and serve. This sauce can be held in a simmering bain-marie.

NOTE : To peel tomatoes and green bell peppers easily, plunge them whole into boiling water. Simmer tomatoes 1 minute; skins will pull away in sheets. Canned Italian tomatoes are usually a superior alternative to the thick-walled fresh ones now swamping the market. They are, of course, already skinned and do not require blanching, but they must be drained. Green peppers should be sliced in half before blanching, and they will need at least 5 minutes of simmering. Sometimes you will need to use a knife to peel the pepper.

SERVES 6

COTES DE VEAU A L'AFRICAINE
(Veal Chops à l'Africaine)

6 thick veal chops (see Note)
1 pound smoked, precooked ham, diced
4 tablespoons butter
1 recipe Corn Fritters (see below)
1 recipe Sauce Africaine (see above)

1. Cut a small slot in the side of each chop. Insert a small knife in the slot with the blade flat (parallel to the counter) and cut a pouch in the chop by rotating the blade inside the chop. Try not to enlarge the opening. A small opening will help keep the stuffing inside the chop during cooking.

2. Stuff each pouch with roughly ⅙ of the ham.

3. Heat the butter in one or two skillets until the foam subsides. Sauté the chops to desired degree of doneness, browning them on both

sides. Serve with Corn Fritters and Sauce Africaine, enriched with degreased pan juices from the chops, on the side.

SERVES 6

NOTE : This is not a traditional combination. The canonical garnish— black or *négresse* potatoes—reflected a childish desire to present an African dish "in black face." Purists may object to the conflation of *haute cuisine* and soul food suggested here. The mixture is in no way jarring, nevertheless, to the unprejudiced palate. It is certainly as "classic" as the prescribed arrangement.

BEIGNETS DE MAIS
(Corn Fritters)

2 cups sifted all-purpose flour
4 tablespoons butter, melted
2 whole eggs, lightly beaten
1 teaspoon salt
Cold water
Oil for deep frying
1 10-ounce package frozen corn kernels, prepared according to the
　　directions on the package, then drained and cooled; or 2½
　　cups fresh corn kernels, cut from the cob, steamed, drained,
　　and cooled

1. At least 1 hour before you intend to fry the fritters, stir together flour, melted butter, eggs, and salt. Add water a little at a time to loosen the dough to the point where it can be stirred but is still firm. Then let the dough rest in a covered bowl at room temperature.

2. Heat oil in a deep-fry kettle until it sizzles when a sprig of parsley is dropped into it.

3. Stir the corn kernels into the dough. Form this mixture into balls of whatever size you please and deep fry a few at a time until golden brown. Drain and keep warm in a low oven until ready to serve.

SERVES 6

✌ SAUCE AIGRE-DOUCE

(SWEET-AND-SOUR SAUCE)

If you should happen to be reading through these pages from cover to cover, do not be alarmed by the apparent eccentricity of the first two sauces and their accompanying dishes. Through an accident of alphabetical order, we have begun with a superficially African and, then, a superficially Oriental sauce. Neither one is, in fact, an oddity within the French sauce corpus. If africaine and aigre-douce are unfamiliar these days, that is a problem of history, not a comment on two sauces which are of the highest quality and former standing. In any case, this sweet-and-sour is thoroughly un-Polynesian.

Serve it with steaks, chops, brains, and sweetbreads.

1 tablespoon seedless raisins
2 tablespoons sugar
2 tablespoons vinegar
½ cup dry white wine
2 teaspoons chopped shallots
1¼ cups demi-glace or thickened jus de veau (page 31 or 35)
1½ teaspoons capers, drained

1. Set the raisins to soak in cold water before you go to bed.

2. The next day, stir the sugar together with the vinegar in a small, heavy saucepan. Boil and continue cooking over medium-high heat until the sugar caramelizes, that is until it turns an appealing light-brown color. Be careful because it can easily burn. Stir and lower heat as the color begins to change. When you have got the color you want, stop the caramelization by pouring in the white wine and stirring vigorously for the next few seconds to lower the temperature of the mixture. If you will feel more confident using a candy thermometer, caramelization begins at 338 degrees; black and bitter disaster occurs at 350 degrees.

3. Having added the wine, stir in the shallots. Bring to a boil and reduce by about one-third.

4. Stir in the demi-glace or thickened jus de veau. Boil for a few moments; then push the sauce through a chinois into another saucepan. Keep hot in a bain-marie. Stir occasionally to prevent the formation of a skin.

5. Just before serving, drain the raisins and add them to the sauce along with the capers. Bring to a boil and serve.

SERVES 6

PAIN DE CERVELLES DE VEAU AIGRE-DOUCE
(*Soufflé of Calf's Brains, Sweet-and-Sour*)

In America, brains are rarely eaten, which is a national mistake. This forgotten "bread" may help to entice your circle into trying a foolishly spurned organ meat. Pain de Cervelles is somewhere between a mousse and a soufflé in method, appearance, and texture. I doubt anyone will be able to tell what it is made of. But they will realize that it is rich, smooth, and delicious. It will not collapse like a soufflé, and most of the work can be done the night before.

1½ pounds (2 pairs) calf's brains
Vinegar
Salt
½ pound unpeeled fresh shrimp
½ cup dry white wine
¼ cup raw rice
2 cups milk
Butter
½ cup heavy cream
3 whole eggs
¼ teaspoon white pepper
½ teaspoon paprika
1 recipe Sauce Aigre-Douce (see above)

1. Wash brains in cold water and leave to soak in several changes of cold water for 2 hours. Peel off the outer membrane carefully. Soak

for another 2 hours in cold water acidulated with 1 tablespoon of vine-gar per quart. Peel away any remaining pieces of membrane and cut away the solid white pieces at the base.

2. Blanch brains in enough boiling water to cover them. The water should be acidulated again with 1 tablespoon of vinegar and flavored with salt, about 1 teaspoon per quart. Slip the brains into the water, reduce heat and simmer slowly for 20 minutes. Drain, and, if you do this the night before, refrigerate the brains in a closed container after they have cooled.

3. While you are cooking the brains, simmer the unpeeled shrimp in water to cover, the wine, and 1 teaspoon salt for 5 minutes.

4. Drain, peel, and devein the shrimp. Refrigerate overnight, if desired.

5. More or less simultaneously with the cooking of the brains and shrimp, you can also blanch the rice. Bring a quart of water seasoned with 1½ teaspoons salt to a rolling boil. Add the rice in a slow stream, stir once, and boil, uncovered, until almost tender, about 12 minutes. Drain well.

6. To finish the rice, first preheat the oven to 250 degrees.

7. Scald the milk. Add the blanched rice to it and return to the boil. Cover and complete cooking in the oven for 30 minutes. Do not stir. When done, drain the rice and press gently to extract excess liquid. Refrigerate, if desired.

8. On the day you intend to serve this dish, preheat the oven to 350 degrees approximately an hour before dinner.

9. Generously butter a 5- to 6-cup soufflé dish. Set aside.

10. Simmer the cream until it reduces by one-quarter.

11. Combine the brains, shrimp, and rice in the blender jar along with the eggs, 2 teaspoons salt, white pepper, paprika, and the reduced cream. Blend to a smooth purée.

12. Pour the purée into the soufflé dish.

13. Set the soufflé dish in a shallow pan of boiling water. Bake in the middle level of the oven for 40 minutes.

14. Remove from oven and let cool for 5 minutes.

15. Set an inverted serving platter over the soufflé dish. Put one hand under the dish and one hand over the platter. Invert dish and platter in one gentle motion in order to unmold the "bread." Pour the sauce over it and serve hot.

SERVES 6

❧ SAUCE BIGARADE

Everyone knows about duck à l'orange, which is served in almost all French restaurants. There are just as many bigarade sauces in circulation—bigarade refers to the Seville, or bitter, marmalade orange that should be used for this sauce—but the classic way, with a brown sauce as base, is best, more complex, never cloying.

Serve, of course, with duck or duckling.

2 tablespoons orange peel cut into thin strips with a vegetable peeler
1 tablespoon lemon peel, prepared like orange peel
3 tablespoons sugar
Juice of 1½ medium oranges
Juice of ½ lemon
3 tablespoons red wine vinegar
Degreased, strained pan juices from roasting 2 4-pound ducks (see below)
1½ cups demi-glace or thickened jus de veau (page 31 or 35)
1 tablespoon arrowroot or cornstarch

1. Blanch the orange and lemon peels in simmering water for 15 minutes.
2. Caramelize the sugar by heating it over medium-high heat with 2 tablespoons water in a small, heavy saucepan until it begins to turn light brown. Then stir constantly to avoid burning and immerse the bottom of the pan in cold water. Should the caramel solidify before you need to use it, reheat gently until it melts.
3. Combine juices, sugar, and vinegar in a saucepan. Bring to a boil and reduce by half.
4. Add pan juices, demi-glace or jus de veau, and the blanched peels. Thicken with 1 tablespoon arrowroot or cornstarch dissolved in ½ cup of the sauce.
5. Bring the sauce to a boil and hold, in a bain-marie, until ready to serve.

SERVES 8

AIGUILLETTES DE CANETON A LA BIGARADE
(*Sliced Breast of Duckling à la Bigarade*)

This recipe was originally intended for the ducklings of Rouen in Normandy. These hapless birds are killed by strangulation instead of by having their throats cut. As a result, their meat has a bloody, gamy look and flavor. Even without such duck flesh, this is still an interesting variation on caneton à l'orange. Officially, one should serve only the breasts, cut in strips. In restaurants, it was no problem to find other uses for the "leftover" drumsticks. At home, it will probably make more sense to serve them as a kind of second meat course.

> *2 4-pound ducklings*
> *Salt*
> *Pepper*
> *Demi-glace or thickened jus de veau (page 31 or 35)*
> *1 recipe Sauce Bigarade (see above)*

1. Preheat oven to 350 degrees.
2. Prepare ducklings for roasting. Remove excess fat from cavity and neck opening. Prick skin all over to allow fat to drain during roasting. Rub the cavity with salt and pepper.
3. Set ducklings on a rack or racks in a roasting pan, with breasts up. Set in the middle level of the oven and roast for 15 minutes. Turn ducklings on one side and roast for 20 minutes. Turn ducklings onto their other sides and roast to desired degree of doneness. This will take approximately 40 more minutes for medium rare, somewhat longer to make the juices run clear.
4. Finished ducks can be held 30 minutes in a turned-off oven with the doors open. Meanwhile, prepare the sauce.
5. As indicated in the Sauce Bigarade recipe, the sauce uses pan juices from the roasting of the ducks. Degrease the juices first. Then deglaze the pan with a few tablespoons of the demi-glace or thickened jus de veau specified in the sauce recipe. That is, pour the demi-glace or jus de veau into the roasting pan, and set over medium-high heat. As liquid begins to boil, scrape the bottom and sides of the pan to loosen

congealed duck juices. Whisk briefly, off heat, and then strain through a chinois into the sauce.

6. While the sauce finishes simmering, carve the breasts away from the ducklings. Slice them lengthwise in strips about ¼ inch wide. Put these strips in the center of a serving platter. Carve the rest of the ducklings into serving pieces and arrange around the breast strips.

7. Pour some sauce over the breast meat. Serve the rest separately.

SERVES 8

SAUCE BONNEFOY

This is exactly the same as a sauce bordelaise except that dry white wine is substituted for red. To prepare, see page 47.

Bonnefoy is especially suitable for broiled red meat or for broiled or sautéed fish.

FILETS DE MAQUEREAU MEUNIERE, SAUCE BONNEFOY

(*Mackerel Fillets in the Style of Ms. Miller, with Sauce Bonnefoy*)

Meunière is a method of sautéing fish fillets in butter, but it is not merely a method of sautéing fish fillets in butter. It also involves a last-minute sizzling effect when beurre noisette (butter heated until it begins to turn brown as a hazelnut—*noisette*) comes in contact with moist parsley and lemon juice on top of the fish. This is rarely done properly, as Elizabeth David has remarked, but when it is, it makes a very nice touch, and it is not at all difficult. By legend, this technique originated in the kitchen of a miller's wife who, presumably, looked out her window at a well-stocked stream. I like to think that this *schöne Müllerin* would sometimes have added a sauceboat of Bonnefoy when her floury husband hooked a strongly flavored fish like mackerel.

> *6 mackerel fillets*
> *Salt*
> *Pepper*

Flour
5 tablespoons butter
2 tablespoons roughly chopped parsley
½ lemon
1 recipe Sauce Bonnefoy (see above)

1. Season the mackerel on the flesh side with salt and pepper.

2. Pour a cup or so of flour onto a plate and dredge the fillets in it. Set them between two sheets of wax paper and press down lightly to make the flour adhere to the fish.

3. Melt 2 tablespoons of the butter in a skillet, over medium-high heat. When the foam subsides, put in the fillets and cook until both sides are crisp and the flesh is just cooked through and flaky, about 3 minutes per side.

4. While the mackerel cooks, blanch the chopped parsley in simmering water for 3 minutes. Drain in a colander.

5. Melt the remaining butter in a small saucepan and continue cooking over medium heat until it darkens slightly, to a nut-brown shade. Remove from heat immediately.

6. Turn out the finished mackerel onto a serving platter. Squeeze a few drops of lemon juice over each fillet. Then sprinkle parsley over them, and pour the very hot prepared butter over the parsley. The parsley should retain a small amount of water from blanching, so that contact with the butter will produce the characteristic foaming effect of the meunière process. This will, of course, be lost on guests unless the fish is presented to them immediately afterward. It is probably best to pour on the butter at the table.

Pass sauce separately.

SERVES 6

SAUCE BORDELAISE

Culinary etymologies are fun to try one's hand at, but it often turns out to be impossible to fathom what strange connections occurred in the mind of the chef who first named the recipe you are interested in tracing to its origins. Bordelaise, for example, means "the sauce from Bordeaux." It begins with a red-wine reduction. Bordeaux is (*pace* Dijon) the capital of red wine. A sauce with red wine logically should be dubbed bordelaise. The trouble is that bordelaise was originally made with white wine (also produced around Bordeaux, but that isn't the point) and the key ingredient in the sauce seems to have been the marrow, because dishes called bordelaise are customarily garnished with rounds of poached marrow. Figure that one out. Or rather, don't bother. Spend the time more usefully on the sauce itself, which, by now you will agree, can appropriately be made with any drinkable red wine, not necessarily one shipped from Bordeaux.

Serve with steaks and chops.

1 tablespoon finely chopped shallots
1 cup red wine
1 crumbled bay leaf
1 sprig fresh or 1/4 teaspoon dried thyme
1/2 teaspoon salt
1 cup demi-glace or thickened jus de veau (page 31 or 35)
1 tablespoon unsalted butter
2 tablespoons beef marrow, diced
1 teaspoon finely chopped parsley

1. Combine the shallots and the wine with the bay leaf, thyme, and salt in a saucepan, and reduce by two-thirds.

2. Add demi-glace or jus de veau, return to the boil, and reduce slightly. Remove from heat and swirl in the butter.

3. Strain through a chinois into a clean saucepan. The sauce should be kept warm in a bain-marie until just before serving.

4. Meanwhile, poach the marrow in a small amount of barely simmering water for 5 minutes. Drain.

5. Just before serving, bring the sauce back to the boil, add marrow and parsley.

SERVES 6

TOURNEDOS RACHEL

Tournedos is a typical French steak sliced from the tail end of a filet of beef. It corresponds to the tenderloin portion of a T-bone steak and is not remarkably different from a filet mignon, its anatomical next-door neighbor. The name "tournedos" is a contraction of the phrase *"tourne le dos,"* turn the back. And therein lies a tale.

The composer Rossini, an unremitting gastronome, grew tired of the same old steak served at the Café Anglais in Paris; so he devised the dish now called Tournedos Rossini (a tournedos placed on a crouton and topped with a round of foie gras decorated with three truffle slices). The manager of the café was shocked when the great man placed his order. He thought Rossini's brainstorm was unpresentable and from then on the dish was served "behind the back" of those who ordered it so as to spare them the horror of looking upon the dish any longer than necessary.

It is, perhaps, difficult to picture quite how this trick of covert service was accomplished, and it is definitely impossible to produce Tournedos Rossini in the United States, where fresh foie gras is unavailable. Tournedos Rachel, on the other hand, is a parallel and practical idea. It substitutes artichokes and marrow for foie gras and truffles. Rachel was the stage name of Elisa Felix (1820–1858), a classical actress of renown and a contemporary of Rossini.

6 small artichokes
2 lemons
¼ cup flour
Salt
Pepper
¼ pound (8 tablespoons) butter, approximately
6 thin slices of white bread with crusts removed
6 filets mignons, or other small, boneless cut of steak
6 rounds of beef marrow
2 tablespoons melted glace de viande (page 30)
1 recipe Sauce Bordelaise (see above)

1. Break the stems off the artichokes. Tear away outer leaves, exposing the artichoke bottoms. Slice off the rest of the leaves flush with the tops of the artichoke bottoms. Trim away all green parts on the underside. Rub the artichoke bottoms all over with the cut side of half a lemon. Reserve.

2. In a nonaluminum saucepan, beat flour together with enough water to make a smooth paste. Then add 3½ cups cold water, 2 tablespoons lemon juice, and 1 teaspoon salt. Bring to a boil, reduce heat and simmer for a few minutes. Add artichoke bottoms and continue simmering for 30 minutes or until bottoms are tender. Cool the artichoke bottoms in their cooking liquid.

3. Trim away the choke and leaf remnants, rinse, drain, and season the artichoke bottoms with salt and pepper.

4. Preheat oven to 300 degrees.

5. Melt 4 tablespoons butter in an ovenproof pan just large enough to hold the artichoke bottoms. Paint the upper side of each bottom with some of this butter and lay them face down in the pan.

6. Place a piece of buttered wax paper, butter side down, on the artichoke bottoms. Bake in oven for 20 to 30 minutes, until the artichoke bottoms are heated through.

7. Meanwhile, sauté the bread slices until golden brown in 2 tablespoons of butter. Drain and keep warm.

8. Sauté the filets (or other cuts of steak) to desired degree of doneness in just enough melted butter to cover the bottom of the skillet (or skillets—you will probably need two to finish all the meat at the same time).

9. While the steaks are sautéing, poach the marrow rounds in a small amount of slowly simmering water for 5 minutes, and drain.

10. Assemble the finished dish on a serving platter or on individual plates. Brush the sautéed bread slices (croutons) with glace de viande. Set each steak on the coated side of a crouton. Center the artichoke bottoms on the steaks. Place a round of marrow in each artichoke bottom.

Pass sauce separately.

SERVES 6

SAUCE BOURGUIGNONNE
(BURGUNDIAN SAUCE)

Here we can be fairly sure that the name of the sauce means what it seems to say. Burgundian sauce does use a generous quantity of the red wine for which the region is famous (although no one should feel compelled to go buy a Chambertin for this purpose), and even Carême's sauce bourguignotte bathes in Volnay, although it also includes eel and crayfish. As we now know it, bourguignonne is one of the most versatile sauces for foods that go well with red wine: steaks, chops, and chicken. When you want to serve it with meat or chicken that has been sautéed, sauté the onions for the sauce separately, then add them to the skillet you used for the meat or chicken (after you have removed the meat and transferred it to a serving platter). Add the wine, deglaze the skillet, and finish the sauce there as indicated below.

1 tablespoon butter
2 tablespoons chopped onion
2 cups red wine
1 bay leaf tied in a bouquet with 4 parsley stems and 1 sprig thyme
*   (or dusted with 1/4 teaspoon dried thyme)*
1 1/3 cups demi-glace or thickened jus de veau (page 31 or 35)

1. Heat the butter in a medium saucepan until foam subsides. Sauté the onion in the butter until it has softened.

2. Add red wine and the bay leaf bouquet. Reduce by two-thirds.

3. Stir in demi-glace or jus de veau. Reduce the sauce by half (to about 1 cup of liquid).

4. Strain through a chinois. Hold in a bain-marie until ready to serve.

SERVES 6

CERVELLES A LA BOURGUIGNONNE
(Brains, Burgundy Style)

A very quick recipe, if you have blanched the brains the night before. The sauce nicely masks the brains' blandness but not their lovely texture.

2 tablespoons butter
1/2 cup pearl onions, peeled
1/2 cup sliced mushrooms
1 1/2 pounds calf's brains, soaked, trimmed, and blanched (page
*   42, steps 1 and 2)*
1 recipe Sauce Bourguignonne (see above)

1. Heat the butter until foam subsides. Sauté the onions until soft-ened. Then add mushrooms, lower heat slightly, and sauté until browned.

2. Meanwhile, cut the brains into ½-inch wide slices. Add them to the browned mushrooms and onions. Pour in the sauce. Bring to a boil, reduce heat and simmer gently for 8 minutes.

SERVES 6

❧ SAUCE AUX CHAMPIGNONS
(MUSHROOM SAUCE)

Haute cuisine can be a wasteful business, but this extremely simple sauce uses a reduced mushroom cooking liquid to flavor the mother sauce. Don't worry, the mushrooms themselves are not thrown away. They're used too. The *grande méthode* can be very frugal.

Sauce aux Champignons is even better if made with wild mush-rooms, but so is everything. Whichever mushrooms you use, serve the sauce with steaks, chops, other small cuts of meat, and sautéed chicken.

½ pound mushrooms, wiped clean
¼ teaspoon salt
Juice of 1 lemon
1 cup demi-glace or thickened jus de veau (page 31 or 35)
3 tablespoons unsalted butter, melted

1. Using a nonaluminum saucepan, plunge the mushrooms, whole, into ⅔ cup boiling water that has been seasoned with salt and acidulated with lemon juice. Boil vigorously, stirring once or twice, for 5 minutes.

2. Drain mushrooms, cut off stems and reserve for making soup another day. This recipe uses only the caps and cooking liquid.

3. Reduce the mushroom cooking liquid to 2 tablespoons. Add the demi-glace or jus de veau, simmer for 3 minutes, and strain through a chinois.

4. Hold the sauce in a bain-marie. Just before serving, swirl the butter into it. Then add as many of the mushroom caps as you wish. Those left over can be served as a garnish for whatever meat you are using.

SERVES 6

ESCALOPES DE VEAU AUX CHAMPIGNONS
(Veal Scaloppine with Mushrooms)

Precious, pounded, thin white veal is a luxury, God knows, but if we don't ever buy it, the American veal industry will shrink to an even tinier mote in a sea of beef. Then, there is the ulterior motive that people as splendid as you and I deserve a scaloppine now and then. Also, think of the time you save . . .

The combination of meat and mushrooms is as old and right as any known mixture. Here it is carried to the highest possible level of purity.

12 veal scallops, pounded thin
Salt
Pepper
2 whole eggs, lightly beaten
1 cup flour, approximately
1 cup bread crumbs, approximately
2 tablespoons butter
1 tablespoon oil
1 recipe Sauce aux Champignons (see above)

1. Season the scallops with salt and pepper.
2. Dip them in the egg, then the flour, and then the bread crumbs. Set them between two sheets of wax paper and press down lightly to ensure that the breading adheres to the meat. This process should be set up like an assembly line. Going from left to right along the counter, you should have a bowl with the beaten egg in it, then a plate of flour, then a plate of bread crumbs, and, finally, a sheet of wax paper. At each stage, shake off any excess coating.
3. Heat the butter and oil together in a skillet (or skillets) and sauté the veal scallops over medium-high heat until lightly browned on

both sides—that's all the cooking they need. This is fast food in the best sense, so don't leave the room or all it lost.

4. Arrange the finished scallops on a serving platter. Garnish with extra mushrooms left from making the sauce.

Pass sauce separately.

SERVES 6

✎ SAUCE CHARCUTIERE

Charcuterie is the art of preparing meat, especially pork, in the form of sausages and other delicacies. Quite properly, then, this is a sauce for pork, a simple variation on the Ur-pork sauce, Robert. Just add pickles to the basic recipe, but you will be especially rewarded if you use the half-sour little French pickles called cornichons.

2 tablespoons cornichons
1 recipe Sauce Robert (page 96)

1. Slice the cornichons into matchsticks.
2. Prepare the Sauce Robert. Add the cornichons to it just before serving.

SERVES 6

COTES DE PORC CHARCUTIERE
(*Pork Chops Charcutière*)

Broiled pork chops with mashed potatoes is not everyone's idea of a special meal. But everyone can have his beef Wellington. I will take carefully cooked (the point of this recipe) pork chops and "muslin" potatoes gladly. With a sauce on the side, this is a company dish.

4 medium potatoes
Salt
9 tablespoons butter
1 cup milk, approximately

8 center-cut pork chops
Pepper
1 cup all-purpose flour, approximately
1 recipe Sauce Charcutière (see above)

1. Peel and quarter potatoes.

2. Add 1 tablespoon salt to enough water to cover the potato quarters and bring to a boil. Put in potatoes and boil until they are almost completely tender, about 20 minutes.

3. Meanwhile, preheat oven to 350 degrees.

4. Drain the potato quarters and set them in a pan in the oven for 10 minutes to dry out excess water. Do not turn off the oven.

5. Push the potatoes through a potato ricer into a mixing bowl. Beat 7 tablespoons of butter into them. Blend well.

6. Scald the milk and beat it into the potatoes gradually until the desired consistency is reached. Taste and add salt if necessary. Cover and keep warm in a low oven or over hot water.

7. Preheat broiler.

8. Pound the pork chops to flatten them. Then rub them with salt and pepper.

9. Melt 2 tablespoons of butter and paint it on the pork chops. After buttering, dredge each chop in flour. Shake off excess and put the chops under the broiler about 3 inches from the flame.

10. Let the chops brown nicely on each side. Cook for 10 minutes per side or until juices run clear or very light pink. If you spread a sheet of aluminum foil over the broiler pan, it will be easier to turn the chops without losing the "breading." Use a flat metal spatula to get under the chops and a turning fork to steady them.

11. Mold the potato purée into a mound in the center of a serving platter. Arrange the broiled chops in an overlapping circle around the potato. Serve sauce separately.

SERVES 6

❧ SAUCE CHASSEUR
(HUNTER'S SAUCE)

Lucky the hunter who comes home from field and stream to find this sauce waiting for him. The combination of ingredients is relatively complex: demi-glace, mushrooms, shallots, white wine, Madeira, and tomato sauce; but the final blend is a full-bodied companion for steaks, chops, and sautéed chicken. It will also go well with a chicken-liver omelette, for a light but not frivolous lunch.

½ cup mushrooms, diced
1 tablespoon butter
1 tablespoon oil
1 teaspoon chopped shallots
½ cup dry white wine
1 teaspoon Madeira
1 cup demi-glace or thickened jus de veau (page 31 or 35)
½ cup Sauce Tomate (page 212)
½ teaspoon glace de viande (page 30)
1 teaspoon chopped parsley

1. Sauté mushrooms in butter and oil until lightly browned.

2. Add shallots and drain off half the fat. Then add white wine and Madeira. Reduce by half.

3. Add demi-glace or jus de veau, tomato sauce, and glace de viande. Stir well, bring to a boil, reduce heat, and simmer for 5 minutes.

4. Hold in a bain-marie until ready to serve. Sprinkle parsley over the sauce at the last moment.

SERVES 6

OMELETTE CHASSEUR
(*Hunter's Omelette*)

To us, an omelette with chicken livers suggests a light lunch or perhaps an after-theater snack. In *haute cuisine,* however, the combination is irrevocably tied, by nomenclature, to the sturdier world of the hunt, and linked, as well, to a noble sauce. If this seems a great fuss to make over an omelette, you should know that the classic repertory did not shun even the fried egg.

9 chicken livers
7 tablespoons butter
1 tablespoon oil
1 dozen eggs
Salt
Pepper
Softened butter
Chopped parsley
1 recipe Sauce Chasseur (see above)

1. Slice chicken livers and sauté briefly—until firm but still pink—in 1 tablespoon each of the butter and oil. (The butter and oil from this step may be used for cooking the mushrooms for the sauce.) Remove the livers with a slotted spoon and set near the stove in 6 equal mounds.

2. Beat the eggs lightly with a fork. Also, beat 1 teaspoon salt and ½ teaspoon pepper into them.

3. Make 6 omelettes, one at a time, as follows:

Heat 1 tablespoon butter in a 7-inch omelette pan until the foam subsides. While butter heats, measure out 6 tablespoons of the egg mixture and beat a few times more.

Pour measured egg mixture into pan, over heat, and count to three slowly. Then shake the pan vigorously, at a slight angle to the burner (handle up), once per second until the egg mass thickens slightly while sliding back and forth against the far side of the pan. This will happen quite rapidly.

Put a mound of chicken liver slices at the center of the omelette.

Then, raise the handle and shake it so that the omelette rolls up into a neat package. Hold over heat for 1 more second to brown the bottom.

Turn onto a plate and rub the top with softened butter to make it glisten. Sprinkle with a little parsley and surround with a ring of sauce.

SERVES 6

❦ SAUCE CHATEAUBRIAND

Like many nobles equipped with an inventive chef, the romantic writer Chateaubriand was able to give his name to a dish created by his employee. It was Chateaubriand's cook, Montmireil, who first thought of cutting a piece out of a filet of beef and serving it grilled with potatoes cut in large cloves and cooked in butter. Apparently the sauce called chateaubriand, with its tarragon and cayenne tang, also once went with the same dish but it was soon supplanted by béarnaise. Regardless, we still have the sauce, which still suits broiled meat but has also been applied, as here, to eggs.

2/3 cup dry white wine
2 teaspoons finely chopped shallots
1 cup demi-glace or thickened jus de veau (page 31 or 35)
4 tablespoons butter, sliced
1/2 teaspoon cayenne
A few drops lemon juice
1 1/2 teaspoons fresh chopped or 1/2 teaspoon dried tarragon

1. Reduce the wine with the shallots by two-thirds in a nonaluminum saucepan.

2. Stir in the demi-glace or jus de veau and reduce the sauce by half.

3. Remove from direct heat and hold in a bain-marie until ready to serve. At the last moment, swirl in the remaining ingredients.

SERVES 6

OEUFS PETIT-DUC
(Poached Eggs Petit-Duc)

The natural-food movement somehow overlooked this recipe, which takes mushroom caps, broils them, turns them upside down, and transforms them into organic egg cups.

Also, this is an invitation to try the professional method for poaching eggs. The cooking takes place in advance and the eggs are reheated at your leisure. In between, you can trim them without rushing.

Vinegar
Salt
1 dozen eggs at room temperature
12 large mushroom caps
3 tablespoons butter, melted
Pepper
6 slices white toast, cut into 12 triangles with crusts removed
1 recipe Sauce Chateaubriand (see above)

1. Fill a large skillet (or skillets) with 1½ to 2 inches of water. Add 1 tablespoon vinegar and 1 teaspoon salt per quart of water.

2. Bring the water to a boil. Break the eggs gently into the water. Lower heat so that the water just barely trembles. Cook for about 3 minutes or until the egg whites have just solidified enough to permit the eggs to be lifted out with a slotted spoon or metal spatula and set in a pan of cold water.

You can poach the eggs all at once or in batches, as you like. The cold-water bath halts all cooking action.

3. Trim ragged edges of the whites with a scissors. It is probably safer to do this while the eggs are still in the water bath.

4. Preheat broiler.

5. Make sure the insides of the mushroom caps are well-trimmed so that they will make smooth cups. Paint both sides of the cup with butter. Sprinkle with salt and pepper.

6. Set the mushrooms under the broiler on a sheet of aluminum foil, concave side up, 4 or 5 inches from the heat source. Broil 5 minutes on each side or until mushrooms are heated through and tender.

7. Set out the toast triangles on a serving platter. Center 1 inverted, broiled mushroom cap on each triangle. Keep warm in turned-off oven with door open.

8. Transfer the eggs from the water bath to a pan of water that is between 120 and 130 degrees. Any higher temperature will cook the yolks further.

9. As soon as the eggs have heated through—test this by lifting 1 out and touching it lightly—lift the eggs out of the water gently, drain well, and set them in the mushroom caps.

Pass sauce separately.

SERVES 6

SAUCE CHAUD-FROID BRUNE
(BROWN CHAUD-FROID SAUCE)

This is one of a family of cold, gelatinous sauces that chefs use to decorate food for buffets. Their work is often formal, elaborate and uninviting. But there is no reason for us non-professionals not to be casual with chaud-froid. Any kind of simple decorative elements, so long as they are bright and will shine through the sauce that holds them, will give a special and possibly amusing effect. For instance, with the lamb chop recipe given here, you might decide to cut out the letters of someone's name and attach one letter to the surface of each chop. At appropriate moments, red meat *en chaud-froid* can become the vehicle for political slogans, birthday wishes, or whatever message you want to transmit.

Naturally, abstract decoration with available vegetable peels and other *comestibles trouvés* is always correct and within reach, provided that your chaud-froid will do its job and gel.

1⅓ cups demi-glace or thickened jus de veau (page 31 or 35)
1 tablespoon glace de viande (page 30), or ½ cup braising liquid
  from recipe below, step 8
2 teaspoons Madeira
Gelatin

1. Combine demi-glace or thickened jus de veau with the glace de viande plus 7 tablespoons water or with braising liquid. Stir well. Add Madeira.

2. Put a small amount of this sauce in the freezer for 5 minutes. If the sample does not gel during this period, dissolve 1 teaspoon of gelatin in the sauce and test as before. Continue adding gelatin and testing until gelling occurs. For directions on the use of this sauce, see below, steps 9 and 10.

SERVES 8

COTES D'AGNEAU EN CHAUD-FROID
(*Lamb Chops in Chaud-froid*)

3 carrots, peeled and sliced in thin rounds
2 medium onions, peeled and thinly sliced
2 tablespoons butter
1/4 pound pork rind, diced, blanched for 10 minutes in simmering water, and drained
1 clove garlic, finely chopped
1 bay leaf tied in a bouquet with 3 parsley stems and 1 teaspoon fresh thyme (or dusted with 1/4 teaspoon dried thyme)
1 rack of 8 lamb chops
1 cup unthickened jus de veau (page 35), approximately
1 recipe Sauce Chaud-froid Brune (see above)

1. Preheat oven to 350 degrees.

2. Sauté carrots and onions in butter until softened. Then spread them across the bottom of a Dutch oven just large enough to hold the rack of lamb.

3. Spread pork rind, garlic, and bay leaf bouquet over the carrots and onions. Then set meat on its side over the vegetables and seasonings.

4. Dilute jus de veau with 3 cups of water for braising liquid. (If more liquid is required in step 6, dilute additional jus de veau with triple its volume of water to produce the necessary amount.)

5. Pour 1/3 cup of the braising liquid over the meat. Then cover the Dutch oven and put it over medium heat until the liquid has reduced to a glaze, that is, until it has almost completely evaporated and has turned a caramel color against the bottom of the pot. Pour in another ⅓ cup of braising liquid and repeat.

6. Add enough braising liquid to come halfway up the side of the rack of lamb. Bring to a boil, cover, and braise in the oven for 50 minutes or until the juices run clear. Baste occasionally.

7. Let the rack cool in the braising liquid. Then lift it out and slice it into chops. Chill chops.

8. Strain and degrease braising liquid. Then reduce it to ½ cup. Strain again, through a chinois, and use as directed above in the recipe for Sauce Chaud-froid.

9. Stir the sauce over ice until it begins to coat the back of a metal spoon.

10. Arrange the chops on a chilled serving platter. Brush sauce over them and refrigerate until the sauce gels. Apply one or two more layers of sauce in this manner. If you plan to decorate the chops, set the decorative elements in the second layer of sauce while it is still liquid. Chill, let gel, and then apply a third layer over the decoration. Let excess sauce gel on a saucer or in a bowl. Then cut it loose and dice it. Distribute diced chaud-froid around the chops. Refrigerate until ready to serve. Set platter over cracked ice on a buffet or at the dinner table, if it will not be served immediately.

SERVES 8

SAUCE CHEVREUIL
(ROEBUCK SAUCE)

The roebuck, or roe deer (*Capreolus capreolus*), is a small, white-tailed deer of Europe and Asia much prized for its meat. Game, in general, holds pride of place among all meats in the French system of gastronomic values. As a result, game appears with greater frequency on menus in France than it does in the United States. American law, moreover, forbids the sale of wild game meat, which means that restaurants in this country must buy their game from game farms and venison ranches. Such game is almost invariably frozen, and, although venison freezes better than most meat, this is yet another reason why Americans who want to taste game at its best, prepared in one of the many sophisticated ways developed over centuries by French chefs, ought to think about making friends with a hunter and cooking his catch themselves.

The game sauces—poivrade, chevreuil, and grand veneur—are the most complex of all the brown sauces, requiring special stocks, marinades, spices and sugar to match the nobility of the meat. But they are not limited only to game. Specially marinated domestic meats and even ordinary roasts will go perfectly with any of them.

1 recipe Sauce Poivrade (page 91)
¼ cup diced, fully cooked smoked ham, or ¼ cup diced game trimmings
6 tablespoons red wine
Dash cayenne
¼ tablespoon sugar

1. Prepare the poivrade in the normal manner, except that you should add the ham or game trimmings when you sauté the mirepoix (page 92, step 1). Use ham for dishes made from ordinary meat, game trimmings with game.

Apply heavy instead of light pressure on the mirepoix when you are pushing the poivrade through the chinois. Do not finish the poivrade with butter. Add the red wine, instead, a tablespoon at a time, skimming between additions. The sauce should simmer during this process, for a total period of 15 minutes.

2. Stir in the cayenne and sugar. Hold in a bain-marie until ready to serve.

SERVES 8

GIGOT D'AGNEAU MARINE EN CHEVREUIL
(Leg of Lamb in Game Marinade)

When game is out of season or unavailable, you can transmogrify an ordinary leg of lamb into venison in a special marinade created for this purpose. The taste and texture of the marinated meat is amazingly like the haunch of a stag but more tender. This is not a gimmick. It is one of the most ingenious inventions you will ever come upon and the results will satisfy the most demanding palates. Obviously, this lamb-turned-deer should be served with a game sauce.

1 6-pound leg of lamb with bone in and skin and fat cut away
1 recipe Marinade C (page 211)
1 recipe Sauce Chevreuil (see above)

1. Put the lamb in the smallest nonaluminum container that will hold it. Then pour in the marinade, which should cover the lamb completely. (To bring up the level of the marinade, you can fill up empty space in the container with small jars filled with water and sealed.) Let stand unrefrigerated for 2 to 4 days. Most American kitchens will be warm enough to complete the marination in 48 hours. You should notice the meat change color, turn tender, and take on the flavor of game. It is a matter of judgment how far this process should be taken. But 4 days should be considered a maximum for marinating American lamb.

If the marinade does not completely cover the lamb, and you can't find a container of the right size to correct this problem, proceed with what you've got, but turn the lamb 3 times daily. In either case, once a day remove the lamb and boil the marinade to keep it from spoiling. Let it cool somewhat before putting the lamb back.

2. Preheat oven to 450 degrees.

3. Drain but do not dry the lamb. Place it on a rack in an uncovered roasting pan. Roast for 20 minutes. During this period, turn the lamb every 5 minutes and baste liberally with the marinade.

4. Lower oven heat to 350 degrees. Lamb will be medium rare (160 degrees on a meat thermometer) after another hour and 15 minutes or so, and it will be well done (170 degrees) after about an hour and a half. Baste occasionally with marinade throughout roasting.

5. Let the lamb rest on a serving platter for a few minutes. Then serve, with Sauce Chevreuil passed separately.

SERVES 8

❧ SAUCE DIABLE

(DEVIL SAUCE)

Sauce Diable can be as devilish as you choose. It all depends on how much cayenne pepper you shake in at the end. A little goes a long way. Serve with broiled chicken.

1½ cups dry white wine
2 shallots, finely chopped
1 cup demi-glace or thickened jus de veau (page 31 or 35)
Cayenne

1. Combine wine and shallots in a nonaluminum saucepan. Reduce by two-thirds.
2. Add demi-glace or jus de veau. Bring to a boil, reduce heat and simmer for 3 minutes.
3. Off heat, season to taste with cayenne. About ¼ teaspoon should satisfy most people.
4. Hold in a bain-marie until ready to serve.

SERVES 6

POULET GRILLE DIABLE

(*Broiled Chicken Diable*)

This is the French answer to barbecued chicken. You roast in the normal manner but finish the cooking under the broiler after painting the chicken with a pungent mixture of mustard and cayenne.

2 2½- to 3-pound chickens
Salt
Pepper
8 tablespoons butter, melted
½ cup Dijon mustard
¼ teaspoon cayenne
2 cups bread crumbs, approximately
12 thin lemon slices
1 recipe Sauce Diable (see above)

1. Preheat oven to 450 degrees.

2. Slit the chickens the length of the back and flatten them slightly. Then rub all over with salt and pepper and set in a roasting pan.

3. Drizzle half the melted butter over the chickens.

4. Bake for 30 to 40 minutes. The chickens should not cook quite completely. Juices from the thickest part of the thigh should run light pink.

5. While chickens are in oven, blend mustard and cayenne.

6. Remove chickens from oven and paint with the mustard mixture. Sprinkle liberally with bread crumbs. Then pour on the rest of the butter.

7. Preheat broiler.

8. Finish cooking the chickens in the broiler, 3 to 4 inches from the heat source. When the bread crumbs have browned and the juices run clear, set the chickens on a serving platter and surround with lemon slices.

Pass sauce separately.

SERVES 6

OEUFS GRILLES A LA DIABLE
(*Broiled Eggs à la Diable*)

The chicken came first; here is the egg version of the same basic idea.

1 dozen eggs
Vinegar
Salt
4 tablespoons butter, melted
1 cup bread crumbs, approximately
Butter
6 thin slices white bread
1 cup grated Gruyère or Swiss cheese
Cayenne
1 recipe Sauce Diable (page 65)

1. Preheat broiler.

2. Poach the eggs in water with vinegar and salt (page 59). Cool them in a pan of cold water. Trim with a scissors and then gently pat them dry.

3. Paint the eggs with butter (or dip them in the butter, if that seems easier to you) and then roll them in the bread crumbs. As you finish with each one, set it on a baking sheet covered with a sheet of buttered wax paper.

4. Slide the sheet of breaded eggs under the broiler at the farthest remove from the heat source. Be sure to leave the broiler door open and leave the eggs inside only long enough to brown the bread crumbs lightly.

5. Meanwhile, toast the bread. Cut each of the slices into 2 triangles. Cut away crusts. Then arrange the triangles on a serving platter. At some point in the middle of this step, the eggs will have to be removed from the broiler. It will not matter if they sit for a few minutes. Do not turn off broiler.

6. Mix grated cheese with cayenne and sprinkle generously over eggs. Then run the eggs under the broiler once more. As soon as the cheese has melted, transfer the eggs to the serving platter, setting 1 on each toast triangle. Serve immediately.

Pass sauce separately.

SERVES 6

❧ SAUCE DUXELLES

Duxelles is one of the standard *appareils* or preparations of French cuisine. It is a way of dehydrating mushrooms, which contain large amounts of water, and preserving them. Duxelles is also an ideal way to concentrate the taste of mushrooms, as you will see when you make this sauce.

La Varenne probably invented duxelles while he worked as chef to the Marquis d'Uxelles. There is also the unlikely possibility that the name comes from the town of d'Uxel in the north of France.

Be that as it may, Sauce Duxelles can be served with almost anything: eggs, steaks, chops, fish, and chicken.

*¼ pound mushrooms (caps and stems), wiped clean and finely
    chopped*
4 shallots, finely chopped
1 tablespoon butter
1 tablespoon oil
¾ cup dry white wine
1 cup demi-glace or thickened jus de veau (page 31 or 35)
2 tablespoons tomato paste
2 teaspoons chopped parsley

1. Prepare the mixture known as duxelles with the mushrooms and all but 1 tablespoon of the chopped shallots. Squeeze the raw mushrooms in a towel to extract liquid, which can be reserved for use in a soup or a sauce. Heat the butter and oil in a skillet until the foam subsides; then add mushrooms and shallots. Cook over medium-high heat, stirring occasionally. The mushrooms will give up their water and darken. When the water has entirely evaporated and the mushroom has browned, remove from heat and reserve.

2. Combine the white wine and the remaining tablespoon of shallots in a nonaluminum saucepan. Reduce by two-thirds.

3. Add the demi-glace or jus de veau, the tomato paste, and the duxelles to the white-wine–shallot reduction. Blend well and bring to a boil. Reduce heat and simmer for 5 minutes.

4. Hold the sauce in a bain-marie until ready to use. At the last minute, sprinkle with parsley.

SERVES 8

POITRINE D'AGNEAU A LA BERGERE
(Breast of Lamb, Shepherdess Style)

Lamb breast is virtually the cheapest red meat there is. But it does not have to be served in humble ways. Deboned, braised, cut in strips, coated with mushrooms and bread crumbs, and run under the broiler, lamb breast à la bergère is a triumph of cook over matter. Shoestring potatoes complete the glorification of an economy cut. The mushrooms in the sauce complement the mushrooms on the meat.

1 cup unthickened jus de veau (page 35)
½ pound carrots, peeled and sliced in thin rounds
3 medium onions, peeled and thinly sliced
4 tablespoons butter for sautéing
1 clove garlic, peeled and finely chopped
1 bay leaf tied in a bouquet with 3 parsley stems and 1 sprig fresh
*   thyme (or dusted with ¼ teaspoon dried thyme)*
¼ cup (2 ounces) diced pork rind, blanched in simmering water
*   for 10 minutes, and drained*
6 pounds lamb breast with bone in
1 cup bread crumbs, approximately
⅓ pound mushrooms, finely chopped and squeezed in a dish towel
*   to extract water*
Oil for deep frying
8 potatoes, peeled, cut in matchsticks, and reserved in cold water
12 tablespoons butter, melted
1 recipe Sauce Duxelles (see above)

1. Stir 2 cups of cold water into the jus de veau.
2. Preheat oven to 350 degrees.
3. Sauté carrots and onions in 4 tablespoons butter until softened.
4. Spread carrots and onions over the bottom of a Dutch oven just large enough to hold the lamb breast. Then add garlic, the bay leaf bouquet, blanched pork rind, and the lamb.
5. Moisten the meat with ⅓ cup diluted jus de veau. Set the Dutch oven over medium-high heat, covered, and cook until the liquid has reduced to a caramel-colored glaze. Add an additional ⅓ cup diluted jus de veau and reduce it to a glaze in the covered Dutch oven.
6. Pour in the rest of the diluted jus de veau. It should come roughly halfway up the meat. Add water, if necessary, to increase the level.
7. Bring the braising liquid in the Dutch oven to a boil; then transfer to the oven, cover, and braise for 1 hour or until meat is very tender.
8. Remove lamb from the Dutch oven, drain and reserve braising liquid, and let lamb come to room temperature under a heavy weight.
9. Degrease braising liquid, strain and reduce to 1 cup in a clean saucepan. Use instead of pure demi-glace or jus de veau in the sauce (see above).

10. When the lamb has cooled, debone it, trim away excess fat, and slice the meat into strips about ½ inch wide.

11. Mix together bread crumbs and mushrooms in a shallow pan.

12. Preheat broiler and begin heating 2 to 3 inches of oil in a deep-fry kettle over high heat.

13. Meanwhile, when the oil begins to smoke, drain and dry the potato matchsticks, a batch at a time, and deep fry them until golden brown. Drain, pat dry, and set in a mound at the center of a serving platter.

14. Dip lamb strips in melted butter and dredge them in the bread crumb–mushroom mixture. Then arrange them in a single layer in a buttered, ovenproof dish or pan. Drizzle with any remaining melted butter and place over aluminum foil on the lowest level of the broiler.

15. When the lamb strips have browned on both sides, after 5 to 10 minutes, arrange them around the mound of potato sticks.

Pass sauce separately.

SERVES 8

SAUCE AUX FINES HERBES
(HERB SAUCE)

Since the entire point of this sauce is herbs, it should not be made unless you have access to fresh ones. In most localities, this will entail growing your own, especially in the case of chervil. Chervil is an annual that flourishes in semishade. Seeds should be sown thickly in early spring and again in late summer. Thin plants so that they are 6 inches apart. Harvest when young leaves appear.

Tarragon is a perennial grown from cuttings; it requires direct sun and can be harvested at any time.

Chive plants are widely available for planting in the early spring, in direct sun. They are perennials. Harvest them at any time.

All three of these herbs freeze remarkably well. If you cannot locate seeds or plants in your area, one of the national plant mail-order houses should be able to help.

Serve the sauce made from these herbs with steaks and chops.

½ cup dry white wine
1 tablespoon whole parsley leaves
1 tablespoon fresh chervil
1 tablespoon chive
1 tablespoon fresh tarragon
1 cup demi-glace or thickened jus de veau (page 31 or 35)
1 lemon wedge

1. Bring the white wine to a boil in a small, nonaluminum sauce-pan. As soon as the boiling point is reached, toss in ½ teaspoon parsley, ½ teaspoon chervil, ½ teaspoon chive, and ½ teaspoon tarragon. (These herbs can all be mixed together ahead of time for convenience.) Remove saucepan from heat immediately, cover, and let steep for 20 minutes.

2. Meanwhile, chop remaining herbs as finely as possible.

3. Strain the herb infusion from step 1 through a linen handker-chief into a clean saucepan. Wring out the handkerchief to extract lin-gering liquid.

4. Add demi-glace or jus de veau to the strained infusion. Blend well and bring to a boil. Reduce heat and simmer for 3 minutes.

5. Hold in a bain-marie. Just before serving, add the remaining chopped herbs and 1 squirt of lemon juice.

SERVES 6

FOIE DE VEAU AUX FINES HERBES
(Calf's Liver with Herbs)

1½ pounds calf's liver, with outer membrane trimmed away
Salt
Pepper
1 cup flour, approximately
2 tablespoons butter
1 tablespoon oil
1 recipe Sauce aux Fines Herbes (see above)

1. Cut the liver into 6 roughly equal pieces.

2. Season with salt and pepper. Dredge in flour and set between two sheets of wax paper. Press down on the top sheet of wax paper to make the flour adhere to the meat.

3. Heat butter and oil together in a skillet or skillets and sauté the liver on one side for 2 to 3 minutes. Turn slices and cook 1 more minute or until juices run pink and the second side is browned.

4. Serve immediately. Pass sauce separately.

SERVES 6

EMINCES DE BOEUF MARIANNE
(*Sliced Beef Marianne*)

Emincés with a good sauce are leftovers in the grand manner. Marianne is the female emblem of France. Or was this dish named, like so many others, after a now-forgotten actress of the Belle Epoque, who knew how to husband her resources without cheating her palate? If so, she appears to have tired of mashed potatoes one day and decided to try frying them. One hopes her theatrical inspirations were as successful.

6 baked potatoes
Salt
Pepper
1 tablespoon chopped chive
2 tablespoons butter
1½ to 2 pounds leftover roast beef or braised beef
1 recipe Sauce aux Fines Herbes (page 70)

1. Peel the potatoes and put them through a potato ricer. Season to taste with salt and pepper and mix in the chive.

2. Heat butter in a skillet until the foam subsides. Put in the the potato mixture. Form it into a flat pancake shape and sauté. Stir the potato up from time to time, and then re-form the pancake so that eventually the entire mass turns golden brown.

3. Cut meat into very thin strips. Put them in a second skillet and pour boiling sauce over them.

4. Put the meat briefly over medium-low heat to warm it up. Do not boil the sauce.

5. Turn the potatoes out onto the center of a serving platter. Form them into a mound. Then arrange the beef, with its sauce, around the potato mound.

SERVES 6

❧ SAUCE GRAND VENEUR
(MASTER OF THE ROYAL HUNT SAUCE)

The most complex of all the brown sauces in this book, grand veneur can be summarized in a phrase as a poivrade with currant jelly and heavy cream. It is made for the big dramatic cuts of game: saddles of venison, haunches of bear. The sauce is fittingly heavy but also sweetened as a counterpoise to the strong flavor of the meat.

There are two roads that lead to a good grand veneur. The first begins with an ordinary poivrade (page 91, omit swirling in butter at the end) and ends with jelly and cream (see below, step 7). In this manner, you can make grand veneur without game stock.

Hunters, or cooks who know hunters, should consider the second method. It begins with a game stock, continues on to a poivrade made from the stock as well as demi-glace or jus de veau, and then finishes with jelly and cream.

Either method provides a very special moment.

2 tablespoons oil
1 large carrot, peeled and diced
1 large onion, peeled and chopped
1 bay leaf, crumbled
2 sprigs fresh thyme pulled into fragments or 1/4 teaspoon dried thyme
4 parsley stems
1/4 pound game trimmings (from deer or other furry animals, not from birds)
9 tablespoons vinegar
6 tablespoons dry white wine
1 cup demi-glace or thickened jus de veau (page 31 or 35)
2 1/4 cups game stock (page 209)
1 1/4 cups Marinade B (page 211)
12 whole black peppercorns
1 1/2 teaspoons red currant jelly (see Note)
1/4 cup heavy cream

1. Heat the oil in a skillet until a parsley leaf dropped into it sizzles. Then sauté carrot and onion in the oil, along with bay leaf, thyme, parsley stems, and game trimmings, until meat and vegetables brown lightly. Drain away excess oil and transfer vegetable-game mixture to a heavy, nonaluminum 4-quart saucepan.

2. Add vinegar and wine. Reduce liquid to a glaze.

3. Pour in demi-glace or jus de veau, 2 cups of the game stock, and 1 cup of the marinade. Bring to a boil, reduce heat and simmer very gently, covered, for 4 hours.

4. In the meantime, smash the peppercorns with a mortar and pestle or with the bottom of an empty wine bottle. Add them to the simmering sauce for the last 8 minutes of step 3.

5. Strain through a chinois, pressing hard on the solid ingredients.

6. Put the strained sauce into a clean saucepan, add the remaining game stock and marinade, and reduce to 1 cup. Skim sauce during reduction. Strain the reduced sauce through a chinois.

You now have a game poivrade sauce. (If you want to use it as is, remove fat and then swirl 1 tablespoon butter into it before serving.) It can be made a day ahead and refrigerated so that fat will solidify at the top and can be easily removed. Or you can remove fat immediately with a spoon and/or paper toweling.

7. To advance from poivrade to grand veneur, first heat the degreased poivrade until it just begins to simmer. While you wait, beat the currant jelly into the cream. Then stir the jelly-cream mixture into the hot sauce. Do not boil this sauce.

SERVES 8

NOTE : The proportions given above for jelly and cream may be varied, especially in the case of a sauce based on game poivrade, when 1 tablespoon of jelly and 6 tablespoons of cream will be appropriate to the greater personality of the sauce.

There is yet a third variation of this sauce, in which the game poivrade receives a jolt of liquid hare's blood at the last minute. I mention this only for the sake of completeness.

SELLE DE CHEVREUIL, SAUCE GRAND VENEUR
(*Saddle of Venison with Sauce Grand Veneur*)

A fish poacher is probably the best place to marinate a saddle of venison. Whatever container you use should be just slightly larger than the saddle, so that you don't need to make enormous amounts of marinade.

Marination is slow, heatless cooking. It tenderizes the meat and flavors it. You will see the color darken and the texture soften up.

Marination is only one way of getting game ready for the oven. Some people hang it outdoors until it gets high. I am not fond of the odor of putrefaction that results, and prefer marination. In any case, game should only be hung when the whole (but eviscerated) animal is still warm from the field. You must not try to hang a frozen saddle of venison bought from a butcher. This is gastronomic and medical folly.

Venison saddle, like other "saddles," is the meat between the haunch and the ribs. It makes a dramatic presentation and is remarkably easy to deal with. The meat is very lean, and it is often larded to prevent drying out during roasting. Larding is hard work, and frequent basting will accomplish the same thing.

> 1 saddle of venison, approximately 5 pounds
> 1 recipe Marinade B (page 211)
> 1 recipe Sauce Grand Veneur (see above)
> 4 pickled pears

1. Put the saddle in the marinade. Even if the container you end up using is too large—e.g., a big roasting pan—you can fill up wasted space with sealed bottles filled with water as ballast. The marinade should ideally cover the meat entirely, but you can get along with less depth if you turn the meat three times a day. Marinate the meat for at least 48 hours. Four days is a maximum. Stop before the meat turns to mush. In heated American kitchens, 2 days should suffice. Each day you should remove the venison, boil the marinade (to keep it from spoiling), and then let it cool before reinstalling the meat. It should be obvious that you are not to refrigerate the marinating venison. If you did that, nothing (or at least too little) would happen.

2. Remove and wash the fully marinated venison. Strain the marinade and reserve for basting and future use.

3. Working with a very sharp, small knife, cut away the outer layer of skin and membrane that seems to hold the red meat wrapped inside it. This is tedious but important work. It entails, additionally, pulling out a large number of sinews. Try to tear the meat as little as possible when you extract them.

4. Preheat oven to 425 degrees.

5. Set the meat on a rack, bone side down, in an uncovered roasting pan. You should figure about 15 minutes per pound from the moment the saddle goes into the oven. But for all weights, brown for the first 25 minutes in a 425-degree oven and, without fail, baste with generous amounts of marinade every 5 minutes. Then reduce heat to 350 degrees. A 5-pound saddle should stay in the oven for another 50 minutes, or until it is medium rare. Venison, whatever your preference in steak, must be medium rare. It is unpleasant when bloody and turns to mutton if it is "well" done.

6. Let the meat rest, while you finish with the sauce. Carve at the table and pass sauce separately. Garnish each plate with ½ pickled pear.

SERVES 8

❦ SAUCE ITALIENNE

The flavors of three herbs, mushrooms, and ham merge with the rich base in this "liquor never brewed" by the banks of the Tiber or Arno. But if I were Italian, I would certainly try to claim this sauce as part of *Italia irredenta*.

Serve with steak, chops, or chicken.

¼ pound whole mushrooms, finely chopped
2 shallots, finely chopped
1 tablespoon butter
1 tablespoon oil

> 1 *cup demi-glace or thickened jus de veau or braising liquid from*
>   *Filet de Boeuf or Artichauts à l'Italienne (page 31, 35, 77,*
>   *or 79)*
> 1 *tablespoon tomato paste*
> 1 *tablespoon finely chopped lean, fully cooked smoked ham*
> *Salt*
> *Pepper*
> 1 *teaspoon finely chopped parsley*
> 1 *teaspoon finely chopped fresh or ¼ teaspoon dried chervil*
> 1 *teaspoon finely chopped fresh or ¼ teaspoon dried tarragon*

1. Prepare a duxelles with the mushrooms, shallots, butter, and oil (page 67). Reserve.

2. Heat the demi-glace or jus de veau or braising liquid with the tomato paste and reduce slightly, by about one-fifth. If you are using braising liquid for this, and you do not have enough to make a full cup, add the necessary amount of demi-glace or jus de veau to compensate. If you have an excess of braising liquid, reduce it to 1 cup.

3. Stir the ham and the duxelles into the sauce and simmer for 5 minutes.

4. Season with salt and pepper.

5. Hold in a bain-marie until ready to use. Sprinkle with parsley, chervil, and tarragon just before serving.

SERVES 6

FILET DE BOEUF A L'ITALIENNE

This can be an extremely elaborate dish, if you make the Braised Artichokes and the Pasta Croquettes that, canonically, are supposed to be served with the beef. But there is no need to do this, although the combination is stunning, for the braised steak is a splendid item on its own. Admittedly a lavish and possibly a perverse way to treat expensive beef, braising in demi-glace produces the quintessential pot roast.

1 large carrot, peeled and very finely sliced

1 large onion, peeled and very finely sliced

2 ounces prosciutto or other uncooked smoked or cured ham, very
finely sliced

1 small rib celery, very finely sliced

1 bay leaf

1 sprig fresh or ¼ teaspoon dried thyme

8 tablespoons butter

½ cup dry white wine

3 to 3½ pounds thick filet of beef or other boneless cut of steak

Salt

Pepper

½ cup demi-glace or thickened jus de veau (page 31 or 35)

1 recipe Sauce Italienne (see above)

1 recipe Artichauts à l'Italienne (see below)

1 recipe Croquettes de Macaroni (page 80)

1. Preheat oven to 325 degrees.

2. Stew the carrot, onion, ham, celery, bay leaf, and thyme together in a covered Dutch oven in order to make the *appareil* known as a matignon. (Matignon is like a mirepoix, but it contains raw ham and the ingredients are sliced very thin, in a paysanne, instead of being diced, in a brunoise.) Begin by heating 4 tablespoons of butter in the Dutch oven (which should be just large enough to hold the meat) until the foam subsides. Then add the other matignon ingredients, as listed above, and lower heat so that the butter bubbles gently. Cover and cook, stirring occasionally, until the vegetables have softened but not browned.

3. Stir white wine into the matignon, bring to a boil, reduce heat and simmer for a minute or so.

4. Spread the matignon evenly over the bottom of the Dutch oven. Then set the beef over it.

5. Drizzle the remaining butter over the beef. Season sparingly with salt and pepper.

6. Cover the Dutch oven and put it in the oven.

7. Braise the meat until very tender, which may take up to 2 hours, or less time, depending on the meat and your idea of tenderness in braised meat. Baste frequently.

8. Remove vegetables and reserve. Discard bay leaf and thyme sprig.

9. Set Dutch oven, uncovered, over medium-high heat and brown meat on both sides. Remove meat to a serving platter and keep warm.

10. Return the matignon vegetables to the Dutch oven. Pour in the demi-glace or jus de veau and bring to a rapid boil. Reduce heat and simmer for 10 minutes; then strain the mixture through a chinois. Degrease as thoroughly as possible and use, as directed, for Sauce Italienne (see above).

11. Put three artichokes at either end of the meat on the serving platter. Arrange croquettes along the sides of the meat. Serve sauce separately.

SERVES 6

ARTICHAUTS A L'ITALIENNE
(Braised Artichokes à l'Italienne)

This side dish can be prepared a day or two ahead.

6 large artichokes
1/2 lemon
4 tablespoons salt
3 tablespoons vinegar
1 medium onion, peeled and chopped
1 medium carrot, peeled and diced
3/4 cup dry white wine
1/2 bay leaf tied in a bouquet with 4 parsley stems and 1 sprig
    fresh thyme (or dusted with 1/4 teaspoon dried thyme)
Salt
Pepper
1/2 cup demi-glace or thickened jus de veau (page 31 or 35)

1. Preheat oven to 325 degrees.

2. Break the stems off the artichokes. Quarter them. Trim the points off the leaves and cut out the chokes. Rub all over with the lemon. Reserve in a bowl of cold water.

3. Bring 8 quarts of water to a boil. Add salt and vinegar. Put in artichokes, lower heat and simmer for 8 minutes, to blanch. If the artichokes float, force them under water by weighting them down with a weighted saucepan or small cast-iron skillet.

4. Drain artichokes.

5. Arrange onion and carrot in a bed on the bottom of an oven-proof casserole just large enough to hold the artichokes in one layer. Place artichoke quarters on top of vegetables. Cover casserole and cook in oven for 8 minutes.

6. Add the white wine and reduce by half over medium-high direct heat. Do not cover casserole during reduction. Then add bay leaf bouquet and a small amount of salt and pepper.

7. Pour in demi-glace or jus de veau. If necessary, add water so that liquid comes about halfway up the sides of the artichoke quarters. Bring to a boil, cover, and return to the oven. Cook for about 1 hour or until the artichokes are tender.

If you intend to use the artichokes right away, drain and refrigerate in a closed vessel. Reheat in the oven just before you serve them. Otherwise, drain and keep warm in the oven.

8. Strain the braising liquid through a chinois. Degrease carefully and use, as indicated, for Sauce Italienne (page 76). Excess braising liquid can be refrigerated or frozen.

SERVES 6

CROQUETTES DE MACARONI
(*Pasta Croquettes*)

You might want to call these fried pasta balls Franco-Italian chow-mein. On second thought, perhaps you had better not, but that is what they are. They are also an attractive and crunchy side dish which is something of a challenge to make successfully, because the croquettes have a tendency to fall apart in the deep fat if they are too moist. If this happens, there is not a guest in 10,000 who will know that the fried noodles he is eating were meant to be served as compact spheres. The taste is the same.

½ pound pasta (any solid noodle-type, such as spaghettini), pre-
pared according to directions on package
3 egg yolks, beaten
3 tablespoons butter, cut into small pieces
1 cup bread crumbs, approximately
Oil for deep frying

1. Drain cooked pasta thoroughly. Cut into sections about 1 inch long.

2. Put a handful at a time into a skillet. Toss them over medium heat to dry them out as much as possible without browning or burning.

3. Stir egg yolk and butter into pasta in a mixing bowl. Try to coat the pasta thoroughly.

4. Form the pasta into balls of any size, or whatever shapes please you—cylinders, rings, etc. Roll in bread crumbs. If crumbs do not adhere well, roll the croquettes in additional beaten egg yolk and try again. Set croquettes on wax paper.

5. Heat oil in a deep-fry kettle until it starts to smoke. Fry croquettes, a few at a time, until golden brown. Drain and arrange on serving platter.

SERVES 6

FOIE DE VEAU A L'ITALIENNE
(*Calf's Liver à l'Italienne*)

In Venice, they do this somewhat differently—without flour, with onions—but the principle is the same: very thin pieces of pink, young liver quickly sautéed and, therefore, sweet. It takes about 1 minute to cook liver this way, so be sure to have the sauce ready in advance.

2½ pounds calf's liver, sliced no thicker than ¼ inch
1 cup flour, approximately
Salt
Pepper
2 tablespoons butter
1 tablespoon oil
1 recipe Sauce Italienne (page 76)

1. Cut away the outer membrane from each slice of liver. Then cut the liver into strips ½ inch wide.

2. Dredge the strips in flour lightly seasoned with salt and pepper. Press between two sheets of wax paper.

3. Heat butter and oil in a skillet until foam subsides. Sauté the liver for about 1 minute, turning so as to brown all sides.

4. Remove liver to a serving platter and serve immediately. The sauce can either be poured over the liver on the platter or passed separately.

SERVES 6

❧ SAUCE LYONNAISE

Classic sources specify that lyonnaise is especially appropriate for leftover meats. It is hard to see why this simple but palatable marriage of demi-glace and a white-wine–onion reduction should be reserved primarily for humble occasions. Perhaps the custom derives from the down-to-earth nature of the people of Lyon, who are the world's greatest gastronomes but utterly without gastronomic snobbery. In any case, the sauce named for their region will suit almost any red meat.

1 tablespoon butter
1 medium onion, very finely chopped
¼ cup white-wine vinegar
¼ cup dry white wine
1 cup demi-glace or thickened jus de veau (page 31 or 35)

1. Heat the butter in a skillet until the foam recedes. Cook the onion slowly over low heat, covered, until softened but not browned.

2. Add vinegar and white wine. Reduce by two-thirds.

3. Add the demi-glace or jus de veau. You may also substitute the strained cooking liquid from Artichauts à la Lyonnaise (page 83) and supplement it, if necessary, with enough pure mother sauce to make 1 cup.

4. Bring to a boil. You may serve as is, or, for an especially sleek effect, skim while simmering for 5 minutes and then strain through a chinois. Hold sauce in a bain-marie until ready to use.

SERVES 6

EMINCES DE BOEUF A LA LYONNAISE
(*Sliced Beef à la Lyonnaise*)

3 to 3½ pounds leftover roast beef or braised beef
1 recipe Sauce Lyonnaise (see above)

Prepare as for Emincés de Boeuf Marianne (page 72, steps 3 and 4).

ARTICHAUTS A LA LYONNAISE
(*Artichokes à la Lyonnaise*)

Vegetable side dishes are, as they say, good for you, and they are good for dressing up a last-minute dinner party where the main dish has to be something sautéed or broiled quickly. These artichokes can be simmered a day ahead, and they produce a fine cooking liquid for your sauce.

6 large artichokes, quartered, trimmed, and blanched (page 79)
½ lemon
4 tablespoons salt } *for preparing and*
3 tablespoons vinegar } *blanching artichokes*
Salt
Pepper
Butter
½ cup dry white wine
¼ cup demi-glace or unthickened jus de veau (page 31 or 35)
1 recipe Sauce Lyonnaise (page 82)

1. Arrange blanched artichoke quarters in a buttered skillet (or skillets).
2. Pour on enough water to come about ¼ inch up the sides of the artichokes. Season with salt and pepper.
3. Melt 2 tablespoons of butter and drizzle it over the artichokes.
4. Bring the water to a boil, reduce heat and simmer gently, cov-

ered, for 30 minutes or until artichokes are tender. Replenish water, if necessary, with more boiling water.

5. Drain artichokes well and keep them hot in a warming oven until ready to serve.

6. Pour white wine into the skillet and reduce by half. Stir in demi-glace or jus de veau, bring to a boil, and strain through a chinois. Use this liquid in preparing the sauce (see page 82, step 3), which should be passed separately.

SERVES 6

❧ SAUCE AU MADERE
(MADEIRA SAUCE)

Served often in restaurants of all levels, Madeira sauce is usually a decoction of inferior sauce base disguised with wine. Good base lightly flavored with Madeira will produce one of the greatest of all sauces. The all-purpose blended Madeira that is most commonly sold will work well in sauces.

Serve with steaks, chops, and ham.

1½ cups demi-glace or thickened jus de veau (page 31 or 35)
2 tablespoons Madeira

1. Bring the demi-glace or jus de veau to a boil. Reduce slightly.
2. Remove sauce to a bain-marie. Just before serving, stir in Madeira.

SERVES 10

JAMBON BAYONNAISE
(*Ham Braised in Madeira*)

In its classic form, this is one of the outstanding dishes borrowed from regional cooking and incorporated into the classic repertory. Bayonne, in the southwest of France, is known for its hams. In truth, these hams come from Orthez in Béarn, but are cured with Bayonne salt.

Nevertheless, the raw ham known as jambon de Bayonne is a delicacy by itself, and doubly so when braised in Madeira. This process also works wonders with ordinary American smoked and cooked packing-house hams. They turn dark in color and honeyed in taste.

The braising liquid you are left with after "madeirizing" an American ham is, unfortunately, too salty to use in a sauce, although it could, presumably, be degreased and preserved to braise a second ham.

Jambon bayonnaise is conventionally served with a sumptuous rice pilaf containing tomatoes, chipolata sausages, and mushrooms. If you can find chipolatas, well and good. Other small sausages will not mar the dish.

1 8- to 10-pound smoked or cured ham
2 cups Madeira
1 recipe Rice Pilaf (see below)
1 recipe Sauce au Madère (see above)

1. Preheat oven to 275 degrees.
2. Trim the ham of almost all its fat, leaving a layer ½ inch thick.
3. Put the ham in a Dutch oven that will just hold it.
4. Pour the Madeira over the ham. Bring the liquid to a boil.
5. Cover the Dutch oven and set in the oven for 2 to 2½ hours. Baste frequently during this time. The ham is done when it is tender.
6. Drain the ham and let it rest for 30 minutes at room temperature or up to an hour in an extinguished oven with the door ajar.
7. Serve with Rice Pilaf. Pass sauce separately.

SERVES 10

RIZ PILAF
(Rice Pilaf)

½ pound (2 sticks or 1 cup) butter
1 large onion, chopped
5 cups chicken stock, homemade (page 102) or canned
2 cups raw rice
3 canned Italian tomatoes, drained, seeded, and chopped
20 mushroom caps, sautéed in 1 tablespoon butter until tender
20 small link sausages, sautéed in 1 tablespoon butter until crusty

1. Melt the butter in a large, heavy saucepan that will hold about 5 quarts. Heat until foam subsides, add onion, reduce heat, cover, and stew until the onion has softened but not browned. In another saucepan, bring the stock to a boil.

2. Take the rice (do not wash or wet it) and pour it in a steady stream into the saucepan, stirring. Raise heat to medium high. Continue stirring rice until it all turns milky. Immediately pour in the boiling stock. Stir once.

3. Cover and cook over low heat for 9 minutes.

4. Mix tomato, mushroom caps, and sausages into the rice. Cover again and continue cooking over low heat for another 9 minutes or until rice is tender but still slightly chewy. Let the pilaf stand, off heat but covered, until any remaining liquid is absorbed.

If you wish to prepare the pilaf in advance, it will keep for hours in a warming oven.

SERVES 10

FILET DE BOEUF DAUPHINE

Proceed exactly as for Filet de Boeuf à l'Italienne (page 77). Use the cooking liquid to make a Sauce au Madère (page 84), supplementing with pure demi-glace or thickened jus de veau (page 31 or 35) as necessary. Garnish with Croquettes Dauphine (see below), instead of Braised Artichokes and Pasta Croquettes.

CROQUETTES DAUPHINE

Mashed potatoes lightened with cream puff dough and then deep fried as airy croquettes.

2 pounds potatoes, peeled and quartered
Salt
10½ tablespoons butter
White pepper
3 whole eggs
4 egg yolks, beaten

10 tablespoons sifted flour
1 cup bread crumbs, approximately
Oil for deep frying

1. Preheat oven to 400 degrees.

2. Plunge potato quarters into boiling, salted (1½ teaspoons salt per quart) water to cover, and boil until tender but still firm. Drain.

3. Set potatoes in the oven, with the door ajar, for a few minutes to dry them out. Then push them through a potato ricer into a mixing bowl.

4. Beat 7 tablespoons of the butter into the potatoes. Season to taste with salt and white pepper. Then beat in 1 whole egg and 4 egg yolks.

5. Prepare a cream puff dough (pâte à chou). Combine ½ cup water, 1 teaspoon salt, and remaining butter (3½ tablespoons) in a saucepan and bring to a boil. Remove from heat and add flour all at once. Stir with a wooden spoon over medium heat until the dough dries out to the point where it no longer sticks to the spoon. It will also begin to leak butter. Then remove from heat once more. Stir in the remaining 2 whole eggs, 1 at a time, blending well.

6. Beat the cream puff dough into the potato mixture. Blend well. You now have an *appareil* dauphine.

7. Divide this dauphine mixture into lime-size spheres. Work with 2 soup spoons and keep dipping the spoons in cold water to clean them. Collect the croquettes on a sheet of wax paper.

8. Roll each croquette in bread crumbs and set them on a clean sheet of wax paper. Sprinkle excess bread crumbs over the croquettes.

9. Shortly before you are ready to serve the croquettes, heat the oil in a deep-fry kettle until it smokes. Then deep fry croquettes a few at a time until they are golden brown. Drain in a bowl lined with paper toweling and keep them hot in a warming oven until you have finished frying all the croquettes and are ready to serve them.

SERVES 6

FILET DE BOEUF DUCHESSE

Proceed exactly as for Filet de Boeuf à l'Italienne (page 77). Use the cooking liquid to make a Sauce au Madère (page 84), supplementing with pure demi-glace or thickened jus de veau (page 31 or 35) as necessary. Garnish with duchesse potatoes (instead of Braised Artichokes and Pasta Croquettes), which are made from the same *appareil* as Croquettes Dauphine (see above). Butter the edge of the serving platter, then either spread the *appareil* over it with your hands or push it on through a pastry bag with a large opening.

Keep the meat separate (i.e., work with an empty serving platter, which must be ovenproof), apply the potato, and then set the serving platter (still without meat) in a 350-degree oven for 5 to 7 minutes to puff and brown the potato ring. When the potatoes have finished, set the meat carefully on the center of the platter and serve. Pass Sauce au Madère separately.

SERVES 6

SAUCE PERIGOURDINE

This is the same as Sauce Périgueux (see below), except that the truffles should be sliced thickly or "turned" into the shape of small olives. Périgourdine is used interchangeably with Périgueux.

SAUCE PERIGUEUX

There is no substitute for fresh truffles. Nevertheless, just as we settle for vicarious (and odorless) sex in books and films, so too, given a desperate appetite for—and a far greater scarcity of—the real, black, aromatic *Tuber melanosporum,* we who are not pig-owning peasants in the valleys of the Lot and the Dordogne, nor wastrel princes, must buy our truffles in cans. Or bottles.

The preserved truffle is a dying whisper of its pristine self, a mummy disintegrating as the millennial linen is unwrapped, a Proustian echo, the gentle thud of a distant cannon. But it is a truffle, and it can be marginally revived by pouring Madeira or Cognac into its canning liquor an hour before use.

The best preserved truffles are the so-called *première cuisson* variety, which have suffered only the first but not the second "cooking" more normally performed on canned truffles. They can be mail-ordered from Société Alimentaire Guillot, 84600 Grillon, France. Order fresh black truffles from Paul Urbani, 130 Graf Avenue, Trenton, New Jersey 08607.

If you do get your hands on some kind of truffle, Périgueux and Périgourdine are the sauces to make. They go with practically everything except fish.

1 cup demi-glace or thickened jus de veau (page 31 or 35)
⅓ cup truffle canning liquor (disregard if using fresh truffles)
3 to 4 ounces truffles, chopped

1. Bring the demi-glace or jus de veau to a boil.
2. Add truffle liquor and chopped truffle.
3. Hold in a bain-marie until ready to use.

SERVES 6

OEUFS POCHES A LA PERIGOURDINE
(*Poached Eggs à la Périgourdine*)

Why, you are asking, does this man waste his precious truffles on poached eggs? Not without reason, is the answer. Because the combination is superb. Because my most transcendent truffle experience was with truffles and eggs. Because the egg does not compete with the truffle, merely gives it a context, a mise-en-scène. And, remember, there will be a sauce.

Furthermore, this is only a suggestion; obviously, if you want to stuff a loin of veal with truffles, we will happily accept your invitation to dinner.

12 thin slices white bread
3 tablespoons butter
12 thick truffle slices
12 jumbo eggs, poached (page 59)
1 recipe Sauce Périgueux (see above) or Sauce Périgourdine (page 88)

1. Cut the crusts away from the bread. Sauté the slices in the butter until golden brown. Keep warm in the oven.
2. Warm 6 plates.
3. Set 2 bread slices on each plate.
4. Put a truffle slice at the center of each bread slice.
5. Place a revived poached egg over each truffle slice.
6. Pour sauce over eggs and serve immediately.

SERVES 6

SAUCE PIQUANTE

Another variation on the basic theme of sauce for pork. This time the white wine/vinegar/shallot reduction-cum-demi-glace melody is decorated with some grace notes in the form of herbs and cornichons, the little French pickles.

⅓ cup dry white wine
⅓ cup white-wine vinegar
1 tablespoon chopped shallots
1 cup demi-glace or thickened jus de veau (page 31 or 35)
1 teaspoon chopped parsley
1 teaspoon chopped cornichons
1 teaspoon chopped fresh chervil, or ¼ teaspoon dried
1 teaspoon chopped fresh tarragon, or ¼ teaspoon dried

1. Combine white wine, vinegar, and chopped shallots in a non-aluminum saucepan. Reduce liquid by half.
2. Stir in the demi-glace or thickened jus de veau. Bring to a boil, reduce heat and simmer for 10 minutes.

3. Hold in a bain-marie until ready to serve. At the last minute, sprinkle in the parsley, cornichons, chervil, and tarragon.

SERVES 6

COTES DE PORC, SAUCE PIQUANTE
(Pork Chops with Piquant Sauce)

The return of the pork chop to your table can be varied with this new sauce, as well as with an almost limitless array of vegetables: raw watercress, or red cabbage braised with a little butter and vinegar and spiced with quartered apples, fried apple rings, potatoes in a hundred different styles, sautéed cucumbers, baked squash, and deep-fried zucchini.

6 center-cut pork chops
4 tablespoons butter, melted
1 cup bread crumbs, approximately
1 recipe Sauce Piquante (see above)

1. Preheat broiler.

2. Flatten the chops by pounding them with a mallet or the bottom of an empty wine bottle.

3. Brush each chop on both sides with butter; then dredge it in bread crumbs and set it on a sheet of aluminum foil stretched over the broiler tray.

4. Run under the broiler 3 inches from the heat source. Broil until juices run clear. Turn once so that both sides brown.

5. Arrange chops on a serving platter. Pass sauce separately.

SERVES 6

SAUCE POIVRADE

Poivrade is the most powerful sauce served with steaks and chops and roasts. It is closely related to a game sauce of the same name: both of them are flavored with crushed whole peppercorns. But ordinary poivrade can be made with normally available materials. A game stock (page 209) is not necessary. On the other hand, ordinary poivrade will go very nicely with the odd cut of venison or the gift parcel of game birds that nonhunters sometimes do receive. For those who have frequent access to fresh game, a recipe for game poivrade is provided here as part of the recipe for Sauce Grand Veneur (page 73, steps 1–6), which is an extension of poivrade pour gibier.

2 tablespoons oil
1 medium carrot, peeled and chopped
1 small onion, peeled and chopped
2 parsley stems
1 bay leaf, crumbled
2 sprigs fresh thyme, pulled into fragments, or ¼ teaspoon dried thyme
3 tablespoons vinegar
¾ cup marinade (page 211 and Note below)
1 cup demi-glace or thickened jus de veau (page 31 or 35)
8 whole black peppercorns
½ tablespoon butter

1. Heat the oil in a skillet until a parsley leaf will sizzle when dropped into it. Then add carrot, onion, parsley stems, bay leaf, and thyme. Sauté until vegetables are lightly browned. Drain off oil.

2. Moisten this mixture (which is called a mirepoix) in the skillet with the vinegar and 6 tablespoons of the marinade. Reduce by two-thirds (to about ⅓ cup of liquid).

3. Stir in the demi-glace or jus de veau, bring to a boil, reduce heat and simmer slowly for 45 minutes.

4. Eight minutes before the sauce finishes simmering, crush the peppercorns with a mortar and pestle or with the bottom of an empty wine bottle and then add the pepper to the sauce. "A longer sojourn in the sauce," says Escoffier, "would be quite harmful, because the pepper would then add too dominant a note."

5. Strain sauce through a chinois, pressing lightly on the vegetables.

6. Add the remaining marinade. Bring to a boil again and skim carefully over medium-high heat while reducing to desired thickness.

7. Strain again. Hold in a bain-marie until ready to serve. At the last minute, swirl in the butter.

SERVES 6

N O T E : The appropriate marinade will vary slightly in content according to the dish for which the sauce is intended. A page reference is therefore provided with the recipe that follows; indications for their use are attached to the marinades (page 211).

COTELETTES DE CHEVREUIL CONTI
(Venison Chops Conti)

6 tablespoons oil, approximately
6 venison chops
6 slices cooked, smoked tongue
2 tablespoons dry white wine
1 recipe Sauce Poivrade (page 91), made with ⅓ the quantity of
    ingredients indicated for Marinade A (page 211)
1 recipe Purée de Lentilles (see below)

1. Heat half the oil in each of two skillets. When it starts to smoke, put in the chops and sauté until they are browned and medium rare, about 5 minutes on each side. Drain and keep warm in a warming oven.

2. Sauté the tongue slices in the same oil you used for the chops. Brown them lightly on both sides.

3. Arrange chops and tongue slices on a serving platter in an overlapping line—chop on tongue on chop, etc. Keep warm.

4. Pour a tablespoon of wine into each skillet and deglaze the

meat juices over medium heat. Pour the deglazed liquid into the Sauce Poivrade.

5. Serve this dish with Purée de Lentilles. Pass sauce separately.

SERVES 6

PUREE DE LENTILLES

There are three usual accompaniments for game dishes: chestnut purée, currant jelly, and lentil purée. Chestnuts are commonly available in the United States only at Christmas time, and they are a chore to peel. Also, since chestnuts are generally imported here from countries whose chestnut trees did not succumb to disease, they are relatively expensive. Excellent currant jelly is available everywhere, but with the astronomical rise in the price of sugar, it is no longer cheap even if made at home. Lentils have gone up, too, but they are still a relative bargain and they are an excellent vegetable source of protein. Perhaps more to the point, they make an ideal taste counterpoint to venison and an interesting alternative to mashed potatoes at any meal.

2 cups lentils
1 tablespoon salt, approximately
8 tablespoons (1 stick or ½ cup) butter
½ cup heavy cream

1. Put the lentils into a saucepan and cover with cold water. Bring to a boil, add salt, reduce heat and simmer until lentils have softened but not turned to mush, about 30 minutes. Add boiling water, if necessary.

2. Drain lentils and put them through a food mill.

3. Cut the butter into small pieces and beat it into the lentil purée. Blend well. Then stir over medium heat to dry out the purée a bit. Do this for 5 minutes.

4. Off heat, stir in the cream. Blend well.

5. Taste and add more salt if necessary.

SERVES 6

❧ SAUCE AU PORTO
(PORT SAUCE)

This is the same as Sauce au Madère (page 84), except that ruby port is used instead of Madeira.

ROGNONS DE VEAU AU PORTO
(Veal Kidneys with Port)

A favorite dish of mine, this is lightning fast. The port tames the kidneys without breaking their spirit.

4 veal kidneys
2 tablespoons butter
2 tablespoons oil
½ cup ruby port
1 recipe Sauce au Porto (see above)
Salt
Pepper

1. Peel away the outer filament covering each kidney. (Occasionally, the kidneys may come to you with a thick outer casing of fat, which must be removed also.) Trim away the clumps of fat tucked into the curve of the kidney. The more you trim, the less you taste later. This gets easier after you have trimmed a kidney or two.

Do not wash kidneys. If they have an unpleasant odor, there is nothing you can do about it except smell the kidneys before you buy them the next time. Do not buy kidneys that have been obviously hacked up by the butcher.

2. Cut the kidneys into ⅛-inch slices. Heat the butter and oil together in a skillet. You will want the highest possible heat in order to sauté the kidneys quickly without toughening them. Nevertheless, the butter must not burn.

3. Put in the kidneys all at once and sauté for 2 to 3 minutes, or just long enough to brown the slices lightly, but not so long that their juices will be released. During sautéing, turn the slices with a spatula to brown all sides.

4. As soon as browning takes place, pour in the port and reduce heat to low. Use a spatula to deglaze the congealed juices on the bottom of the pan.

5. Add Sauce au Porto and, if necessary, salt and pepper. Serve immediately.

Rice makes an ideal accompaniment to this dish.

SERVES 6

SAUCE ROBERT

A bottled version of this sauce is sold in fancy food stores. It bears no resemblance to real Robert, which is one of the oldest sauces on record and one of the best. For centuries, Robert has been *the* pork sauce.

1 tablespoon butter
1 medium onion, peeled and finely chopped
2/3 cup dry white wine
1 cup demi-glace or thickened jus de veau (page 31 or 35)
1/4 teaspoon sugar
1 1/2 teaspoons Dijon mustard

1. Heat the butter in a skillet until foam subsides. Add onion and sauté until softened but not browned.

2. Add the white wine and reduce by two-thirds.

3. Add the demi-glace or jus de veau, bring to a boil, reduce heat and simmer for 10 minutes.

4. Strain the sauce through a chinois or transfer directly to a bain-marie. Hold there until ready to use. At the last minute, stir in the sugar and mustard.

SERVES 6

ROTI DE PORC, SAUCE ROBERT
(Roast Pork with Robert Sauce)

There are many theories about the best way to roast a loin of pork: in casseroles, in open pans, browned on top of the stove, browned in the oven. The method that follows is certainly simple and has always produced a juicy, delicious roast in our house, without the *Sturm und Drang* gone through by some people to keep the roast from drying out. If there is a secret involved, it must be a combination of quick searing at high temperature, slow cooking thereafter, and what may seem on first glance to be an excessive amount of garlic. Don't blanch at the number of cloves; they lose their ferocity in the oven. Apparently, it sweats away and leaves only a pleasing aroma.

1 3½-pound pork roast with bone in
Salt
Pepper
4 cloves garlic, peeled and sliced
Rosemary
1 recipe Sauce Robert (see above)
¼ cup dry white wine

1. Preheat oven to 425 degrees.
2. Rub roast all over with salt and pepper.
3. Jab it in all the fleshy places with a sharp-pointed knife to a depth of about ½ inch. Use your fingers to force a slice of garlic into each incision as far as it will go. The meat will close over the garlic and hold it in.
4. Set the roast, bone side down, on a rack in an uncovered roasting pan. Sprinkle lightly with rosemary.
5. Set the roast in the oven and keep your eye on it. After 10–15 minutes, it should have browned nicely. When this happens, reduce heat to 325 degrees, baste, and continue roasting until the roast is done. This should take approximately another hour and 45 minutes. The tests for doneness are a reading of 180 degrees on a meat thermometer and/or clear-running juices. Baste the roast often during roasting.

6. Set the finished roast on a serving platter to rest, while you de-grease the drippings in the roasting pan and finish the sauce.

7. Deglaze the roasting pan over medium heat with the dry white wine and add to sauce after straining.

8. Carve the roast at the table. Pass sauce separately.

Purée de Lentilles would make an excellent side dish (page 94).

SERVES 6

White
Sauces

Sauces Derived from Ordinary Velouté

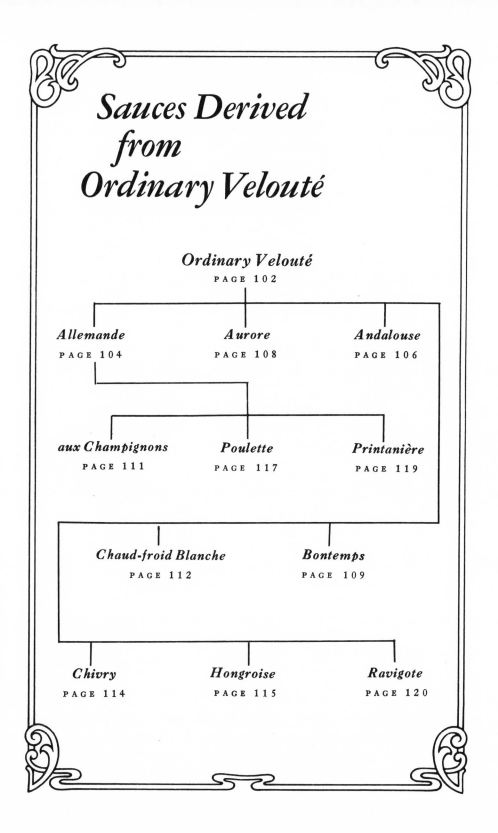

Ordinary Velouté
PAGE 102

Allemande
PAGE 104

Aurore
PAGE 108

Andalouse
PAGE 106

aux Champignons
PAGE 111

Poulette
PAGE 117

Printanière
PAGE 119

Chaud-froid Blanche
PAGE 112

Bontemps
PAGE 109

Chivry
PAGE 114

Hongroise
PAGE 115

Ravigote
PAGE 120

❧ FOND BLANC ET SAUCE VELOUTE ORDINAIRE

(ORDINARY WHITE STOCK AND ORDINARY VELOUTE)

If you have made demi-glace already, then velouté, the great white mother, will be child's play for you. Velouté needs no endless skimming, only an hour and a half. It uses a stock without browned meats. The roux is done in a few minutes.

Velouté, in fact, is probably the most practical mother sauce with which to begin your career as a *saucier*. It is relatively easy, and it is the threshold to a large number of fine smaller sauces.

3 pounds veal shoulder, with bones cut into 3-inch sections
4½ pounds veal shank, with bones cut into 3-inch sections
4½ pounds chicken backs, necks, giblets, and carcasses
½ pound carrots, peeled and sliced in rounds
4 medium onions, peeled and thinly sliced
1 large leek, washed carefully, trimmed (to eliminate tough green leaves), and thinly sliced
2 bay leaves tied in a bouquet with 5 parsley stems and 2 sprigs fresh thyme (or dusted with ½ teaspoon dried thyme)
1 large rib celery, thinly sliced
20 tablespoons (2½ sticks) unsalted butter
3 cups plus 6 tablespoons (¾ pound) sifted flour

1. Cut the meat away from the veal bones. Tie it up in a bundle and put it in the stock pot.

2. Split and splinter the bones with a cleaver. This step is optional (see directions for splintering, page 37).

3. Put bones in the stock pot.

4. Pour in 7 quarts of cold water. Make sure that the pot straddles as many burners as possible, cover it, and bring to a boil. Then skim carefully and add all remaining ingredients except butter and flour.

5. Bring to a boil again, reduce heat and simmer slowly for 3 hours, uncovered.

6. Remove all solid ingredients from the stock. Reserve the meats; they can be ground up to make patties or croquettes.

7. Strain liquid through a chinois. Let it cool, *uncovered,* and then remove the layer of fat that has risen to the top. This is easier if you refrigerate the stock, because the fat will then solidify.

8. The fat-free stock is known as fond blanc ordinaire or ordinary white stock. It is used as a separate ingredient in many recipes and should be kept on hand, frozen. Also, a quart of it should be reduced to make glace de viande blonde, a cousin of dark glace de viande (page 30), which is prepared and stored in exactly the same way.

This recipe is designed to produce about 5 quarts of fond blanc or white stock, which will produce 5 quarts of ordinary velouté when it is thickened with roux (see final steps of this recipe). However, you might also want to operate as follows: Keep 1½ quarts as stock, reduce 1 quart to glace de viande blonde, and thicken only 2½ quarts. If so, use half the butter and flour specified above for the roux. Or you could double the quantities of all ingredients except the butter and flour and end up with a gallon of stock, a quart for glace de viande blonde, and 5 quarts of velouté, the amount intended below.

9. For velouté: Bring 5 quarts stock and 2 cups cold water to a boil.

10. Meanwhile, make a blonde roux. Melt the butter in a heavy skillet. When the foam subsides, stir in the flour rapidly with a flat wooden spatula or a wire whisk. Reduce heat to medium. Continue to stir every couple of minutes until the roux turns light yellow. The taste of raw flour should have disappeared. Transfer roux to a mixing bowl so that it does not continue cooking.

11. The standard rule for combining roux and stock for velouté is: Add hot roux to cold stock and cold roux to hot stock. The idea is to avoid lumps. Therefore, let the roux cool to room temperature (refrigerate it briefly if the stock is already boiling) before whisking it into the boiling stock.

12. When roux is well combined with stock, reduce heat and simmer for 1½ hours. Skim frequently.

13. Strain the sauce through a chinois and cool, uncovered.

14. Freeze in 1- or 2-cup containers.

MAKES 5 QUARTS (20 CUPS)

✺ SAUCE ALLEMANDE
(GERMAN SAUCE)

Escoffier included this egg-bound velouté among the mother sauces, because it is the basis of many other sauces. If we were to follow him in this decision, it would imply that we would then make up large quantities of allemande in advance and freeze it. But there is no great advantage in this for a private individual, since the amount of time necessary for converting velouté to allemande is small, and the loss of versatility after the transformation of so much velouté would be significant.

I am also departing from Escoffier's counsel in another matter. He tried to suppress the name of the sauce because of hostile feelings to Germany. Since the sauce was German in name only, he proposed renaming it sauce parisienne or sauce blonde. This culinary riposte to the armies of Bismarck and Kaiser Wilhelm II did less even than the Maginot Line to keep the Teutonic menace at bay. And so, in the era of the Common Market, it seems sensible to restore the old label.

Allemande, then, is thickened with egg yolks, but because it has already been thickened with flour at the velouté stage, it can be boiled after the yolks are added. They will not scramble; the flour keeps this from happening. It is essential, however, that all ingredients be cold when you start, since gradual heating of the yolks is also crucial.

½ cup ordinary white stock (page 102, steps 1–8)
1 extra-large egg yolk (or 1½ large yolks)
White pepper
Dash of nutmeg
A few drops of lemon juice
1 cup mushroom cooking liquid (page 209), reduced to ¼ cup
1 cup ordinary velouté (page 102)
1 tablespoon butter

1. Beat together all the ingredients, except the velouté and the butter, in a heavy, nonaluminum saucepan.
2. Stir in the velouté.

3. Bring to a boil and reduce over high heat by one-third, or until the sauce coats a wooden spatula or spoon thickly. Stir occasionally during reduction to keep sauce from sticking to the bottom of the saucepan.

4. Strain through a chinois and hold in a bain-marie until ready to use. Stir occasionally to prevent the formation of a skin on the surface.

5. At the last minute, swirl in the butter.

SERVES 6

OEUFS VIROFLAY
(Eggs Viroflay)

Viroflay is a suburb of Paris near Versailles. Its name became synonymous with spinach, just as that of Argenteuil became a code word on menus for asparagus.

Eggs Viroflay is a pretty dish, in which eggs and spinach are poached together in baba molds. You end up with a green and white composition—a column of spinach enclosing an egg. This is one of those culinary "feats" that look harder than they are. Another point in its favor—aside from the well-known taste affinity of spinach and eggs—is that it lets you get some extra use out of your baba molds. Or, if you didn't have any before, it will give you an excuse to buy some of these inexpensive little metal cylinders so that you can also try your hand at babas au rhum when the mood assails you.

10 ounces spinach, thoroughly washed
Salt
4 tablespoons butter, approximately
6 whole eggs
6 slices white bread, thinly cut and toasted
1 recipe Sauce Allemande (see above)

1. Blanch the spinach in lightly salted, boiling water for 2 minutes, then drain.

2. Heat 3 tablespoons of the butter in a skillet until the foam recedes. Add the spinach, cover, reduce heat and simmer until just tender.

3. Butter the insides of 6 half-cup-capacity baba molds. Line them each with about ⅙ of the spinach. Press the spinach in place so that it leaves a space for an egg.

4. Crack one egg into each mold.

5. Stand the molds in a skillet containing enough simmering water to come two-thirds of the way up the sides of the molds.

6. Poach at a slow simmer until the egg whites have solidified, about 15 minutes. Timing will vary according to the original temperatures of the ingredients and the depth of the water.

7. Cut the toast slices into large circles. Set the toast rounds on small plates.

8. Remove the molds from the water with tongs. Run a thin-bladed knife around the sides of the Oeufs Viroflay. Then invert them over the toast rounds and rap sharply on the bottom of the molds to unmold them.

9. Pour sauce over the eggs and serve immediately.

SERVES 6

SAUCE ANDALOUSE
(ANDALUSIAN SAUCE)

It may amuse you to know that purists would braise the peppers for this tomatoed velouté. In fact, they would blanch them first, then braise them in white stock on a bed of other vegetables. Perhaps some day I may try it that way, too. For the moment, sautéing will just have to do.

Serve Sauce Andalouse with eggs, fish, and chicken.

1 cup ordinary velouté (page 102)
2 tablespoons tomato paste
1 clove garlic, crushed
2 tablespoons peeled, seeded, and diced red (or, in a pinch, green)
*   bell pepper, sautéed in 1 tablespoon butter until softened*
1½ teaspoons chopped parsley

1. Reduce the velouté to ¾ cup in a heavy, nonaluminum saucepan.

2. Whisk in the tomato paste, garlic, and the diced and sautéed pepper. Hold in a bain-marie until ready to serve. At the last minute, sprinkle with parsley.

SERVES 6

POULARDE A L'ANDALOUSE
(Andalusian Chicken)

A roast chicken stuffed with rice pilaf that has itself been garnished with mushrooms, sausages, and tomatoes.

1 4½- to 5-pound chicken or capon
1 recipe Rice Pilaf (page 85)
Paprika
4 tablespoons butter
1 large onion, peeled
1 bay leaf tied in a bouquet with 3 parsley stems and 1 sprig fresh
*   thyme (or dusted with ¼ teaspoon dried thyme)*
1 recipe Sauce Andalouse (see above)

1. Preheat oven to 350 degrees.

2. Stuff the chicken with as much pilaf as it will hold. As you put in the pilaf, season it with paprika. Close up the chicken's cavity with trussing needles and then truss the chicken for roasting. Reserve excess pilaf in a covered saucepan set in a bain-marie. Add a small amount of water if it looks dry.

3. Heat the butter in a small Dutch oven (one just large enough to hold the chicken) until the foam recedes. Brown the chicken in the butter on all sides.

4. Add the onion and the bay leaf bouquet, cover the pot, and cook in the oven for about 45 minutes or until juices run clear from the thickest part of the thigh.

5. Serve with remaining pilaf. Pass sauce separately.

SERVES 6

🜲 SAUCE AURORE

Aurora is the Latin word for dawn, which, as Homer has taught us, is best described as rosy-fingered. (The translation is hokey and does not come up to the alliteration, rhyme, or polysyllabic swing of the original: *rhododaktylos Eos*.) That, at any rate, is the allusion intended by the name of this pink-red mixture of velouté and tomato.

Serve with eggs, chicken, and sweetbreads.

1 cup ordinary velouté (page 102)
1 tablespoon tomato paste, approximately
1 tablespoon butter

1. Heat the velouté. Then stir in the tomato paste gradually until you obtain the best approximation you can of a roseate dawn.
2. Hold the sauce in a bain-marie until ready to serve. At the last minute, swirl in the butter.

SERVES 6

POULARDE A L'AURORE
(*Chicken à l'Aurore*)

You are about to cook a giant quenelle inside a chicken. This is actually easier than poaching little quenelles (featherweight dumplings, see page 144) in the open air. As an added attraction, this quenelle will be made from an old-fashioned veal forcemeat called a godiveau, and it will be colored with tomato paste to match the sauce. The cooked godiveau, scooped out in spoonfuls when you serve the chicken, becomes the garnish for the dish.

½ pound lean veal, ground
½ pound suet (beef-kidney fat), finely chopped
1 whole egg
1 egg yolk
1 teaspoon salt, approximately
¼ teaspoon pepper, approximately

Nutmeg
1 tablespoon tomato paste
3/4 cup heavy cream
1 4 1/2- to 5-pound chicken or capon
*5 to 6 cups chicken stock, approximately, homemade (page 122) or
  canned*
1 recipe Sauce Aurore (see above)

1. Beat together the veal, suet, whole egg, egg yolk, salt, pepper, a trace of nutmeg, and the tomato paste in a mixing bowl. Put through a food mill. Then beat in the heavy cream little by little. This is a godiveau.

2. Preheat the oven to 350 degrees.

3. Stuff the chicken with the godiveau. Sew up the cavity or truss it tightly with trussing needles. If you leave a significant opening, the godiveau will leak out. A trickle is probably inevitable.

4. Pour the chicken stock into a Dutch oven. The Dutch oven should just hold the chicken. The chicken stock should be of a sufficient amount to cover the chicken. Bring the stock to a boil. Put in the chicken and transfer to the oven. Cover and poach for 45 minutes or until the juices run clear from the thickest part of the thigh. By then the godiveau will have solidified.

5. Remove the chicken (reserve the stock for future use after straining) and set on a serving platter. Nap with some of the sauce. Pass the rest separately.

SERVES 6

SAUCE BONTEMPS

This sounds like a cheerful sauce—and it is—but the name probably does not refer to the happy glow induced by the reduction of hard cider and onion mixed with velouté and flavored with paprika and mustard. The most likely explanation is that it commemorates the *nom de plume* of Roger de Collerye (1470?–1540?), the French lyric poet. As Roger Bontemps, he organized a society of bons vivants, whose president was called *Abbé des Fous,* the Fools' Abbot.

Whatever the etymology, Sauce Bontemps goes well with steaks, chops, and broiled chicken.

3 tablespoons butter
1 tablespoon finely chopped onion
Salt
Paprika
¾ cup hard cider
¾ cup ordinary velouté (page 102)
1 tablespoon Dijon mustard

1. Heat 1 tablespoon of the butter in a nonaluminum saucepan. When the foam recedes, add the onion and sauté until softened but not browned.

2. Off heat, season to taste with salt and paprika. Then add cider and reduce by two-thirds.

3. Stir in the velouté, bring to a boil, and remove from direct heat.

4. Hold in a bain-marie until ready to use. At the last minute, stir in the remaining butter and the mustard.

SERVES 6

COTES DE PORC A LA FLAMANDE
(*Pork Chops, Flemish Style*)

Pork chops with apples for a sauce with cider.

6 thick pork chops
Salt
Pepper
3 tablespoons butter
1½ pounds eating apples, peeled, cored, and thickly sliced
1 recipe Sauce Bontemps (see above)

1. Preheat the oven to 300 degrees.

2. Rub the pork chops with salt and pepper on both sides.

3. Heat the butter in a skillet, and, when the foam subsides, sauté the chops until they have browned on both sides.

4. Arrange them in a single layer in an uncovered, ovenproof dish on a bed of apple slices.

5. Cook in the middle level of the oven for about 50 minutes, or until the chops' juices run clear and the apple slices are tender. Serve from the dish. Pass sauce separately.

SERVES 6

SAUCE AUX CHAMPIGNONS
(WHITE MUSHROOM SAUCE)

Sautéed mushrooms turn brown, but this is a white sauce; the mushrooms are prepared à blanc, in specially treated water, so that they do not darken. Then they go into a rich allemande sauce, with their cooking liquid, to enrich it further.

Serve with chicken.

1 teaspoon oil
1/2 teaspoon flour
1/4 teaspoon lemon juice
1/8 teaspoon salt
1/4 pound mushrooms, wiped clean
1 recipe Sauce Allemande (page 104)

1. Mix 1/2 cup water with oil, flour, lemon juice, and salt. Bring to a boil in a nonaluminum saucepan. Add mushrooms, reduce heat and simmer slowly for 10 minutes.

2. Drain mushrooms. Cut away stalks and discard. Reserve caps.

3. Bring the mushroom cooking liquid back to a boil and reduce by two-thirds.

4. Stir the allemande into the mushroom liquid. Bring to a boil, reduce heat and simmer for 3 minutes.

5. Hold in a bain-marie until ready to use, stirring occasionally. At the last minute, add half the mushroom caps. Reserve the rest as a garnish for whatever dish you serve the sauce with.

SERVES 6

POULARDE AUX CHAMPIGNONS A BLANC
(*Chicken with Blanched Mushrooms*)

1 4½- to 5-pound chicken or capon
5 to 6 cups chicken stock, homemade (page 122) or canned
1 recipe Sauce aux Champignons (see above)

1. Poach the chicken in the stock (page 109, steps 2 and 4; disregard references to godiveau and trussing).
2. Place drained chicken on a serving platter. Nap with some of the sauce. Garnish with the mushroom caps reserved from making the sauce.

SERVES 6

SAUCE CHAUD-FROID BLANCHE
(WHITE CHAUD-FROID SAUCE)

Like brown chaud-froid, this is a vehicle for the decoration of foods on cold buffets. White and opaque, it provides an elegant background for your vegetable designs. Chaud-froid is usually associated with creaky, formal occasions, but any sort of picture or message is possible, given imagination, a knife, and a palette of pimentos, olives, and green pepper strips. Despite the technical difficulty of working with the sauce, you have a real opportunity here to exercise your creative faculties, to use a method normally reserved for professionals in your own way.

Serve with chicken, eggs, brains, and sweetbreads.

1⅓ cups ordinary velouté (page 102)
1 cup chicken stock, homemade (page 122) or canned
⅓ cup heavy cream
1 package gelatin, approximately

1. Reduce the velouté in a heavy, nonaluminum saucepan. During

the reduction, whisk in the chicken stock and 2 tablespoons of the heavy cream. Eventually, this mixture should reduce down to about 1⅔ cups. Stir or whisk constantly during reduction.

2. Strain through a chinois and then whisk in the remaining heavy cream, off heat.

3. When the sauce has cooled to room temperature, paint a thin layer on a chilled plate. Refrigerate the plate briefly to see if the sauce gels easily. If a solid gel has not been produced, reheat the sauce and stir in the package of gelatin. Heat until the gelatin has completely dissolved. Cool. Chill sauce until just barely pourable. It is now ready to use.

SERVES 6

CHAUD-FROID DE VOLAILLE
(*Chaud-froid of Chicken*)

1 4½- to 5-pound chicken or capon
5 to 6 cups chicken stock, homemade (page 122) or canned
1 recipe Sauce Chaud-froid Blanche (see above)
Thin vegetable strips and leaves for decoration

1. Poach the chicken in the stock in a preheated 350-degree oven (page 109, steps 2 and 4; disregard references to godiveau and trussing).

2. Let the chicken cool in its poaching liquid. Then cut it into serving pieces. Carefully remove the skin and discard. Chill the chicken pieces.

3. Pour a thin layer of sauce over the bottom of a chilled serving platter. Refrigerate until gelled.

4. Arrange chicken pieces on serving platter. Paint them with sauce. Chill until gelled. Continue coating the chicken with sauce until you use up all the sauce.

5. Before the last layer of sauce sets, decorate by laying vegetable slivers and lozenges on it in the design you have chosen. Chill until ready to serve.

6. Set serving platter over crushed ice if this dish is going to be part of a buffet. Otherwise, serve as is.

SERVES 6

❧ SAUCE CHIVRY

Mixed herbs steeped in wine give this sauce part of its special "garden-variety" flavor. The basic velouté is also mixed with a Chivry butter—more herbs blended with butter. The idea of injecting butter with all manner of flavor essences is an ingenious way of storing tastes in the refrigerator. Just as mother sauces enable the cook to put meat essences in the bank, so the compound butters like Chivry permit you to do the chopping and blending and straining of vegetable, herbal, and other substances in advance. At the last minute, they can be simply melted into a sauce. A selection of these useful butters, which can be employed as sauces in their own right, will be found beginning on page 192.

Serve with eggs, chicken, and lamb.

1 cup dry white wine
1 pinch each of fresh chervil, parsley, tarragon, and chive (see
Note)
1½ cups ordinary velouté (page 102)
1 recipe Chivry Butter (page 192)

1. Boil the wine in a nonaluminum saucepan for 3 minutes. Toss in the herbs. Cover and remove from heat and let stand for 10 minutes. Then strain the infusion through a dish towel and squeeze out the moisture that remains in the herbs into the strained infusion. Discard herbs.

2. Bring the velouté to a boil in a nonaluminum saucepan. Add the infusion. Return to the boil and reduce to desired consistency if thin.

3. Hold in a bain-marie until ready to use. Swirl in the Chivry Butter at the last moment.

SERVES 8

NOTE : If you happen to have a bit of purslane on hand, use it too. Alternatively, if you are unable to find one or more of these herbs, compensate by increasing the amount of the others accordingly. This sauce should not be done with dried herbs. Frozen fresh herbs will work quite satisfactorily.

GIGOT D'AGNEAU CHIVRY
(Leg of Lamb Chivry)

Roasted meat inevitably shrinks and loses weight. This is more than a pity with the price of large roasting cuts at ever-mounting levels. Yet there is an undoubted benefit for the cook in a big piece of meat that "cooks itself." But how to have convenience without shrinkage or the large expenditure of power necessitated by an oven? One answer, if you have a leg of lamb and an herb garden, is to poach the lamb and serve it with Sauce Chivry. Poach a lamb? Indeed. The meat stays very juicy and you serve virtually the same amount of it as you've paid for. Also, the energy required to simmer water is minimal.

1 6-pound leg of lamb, with all but a thin layer of fat trimmed off
Salt
Flour
1 recipe Sauce Chivry (see above)

1. Fill a large roasting pan with enough water to cover the lamb. Bring to a boil.
2. Rub the lamb all over with salt. Roll it in flour, shake off excess, and then tie up the lamb, completely and tightly, in a clean dish towel. (If one towel is not big enough, use two and overlap them.)
3. When the water boils, add 2 tablespoons salt. Then put in the lamb. Return to the boil, reduce heat and simmer very gently for 90 minutes. Maintain the water level with boiling water, if necessary.
4. Remove towel, drain the lamb, and serve. Pass sauce separately.

SERVES 8

SAUCE HONGROISE
(HUNGARIAN SAUCE)

If you use real Hungarian paprika to color this Hungarian sauce, you will create a feisty, pungent pink liquid. Non-Magyar, sweet paprika will add color without sharpness. Either method has its points. Also, "pink" may give the wrong idea of what hongroise will look like. Perhaps orange-red is more accurate.

Serve with eggs, chicken, steaks, chops, brains, and sweetbreads.

2 tablespoons butter
1 small onion, peeled and chopped
1 cup ordinary velouté (page 102)
1 pinch salt
Paprika

1. Heat 1 tablespoon of the butter in a heavy, nonaluminum saucepan until the foam subsides. Add the onion and sauté until softened but not browned.

2. Stir in the velouté. Season with salt. Then whisk in paprika gradually until the color of the sauce turns light pink (or orange-red or rose or whatever shade pleases you). Boil for 2 to 3 minutes, stirring.

3. Strain through a chinois. Hold in a bain-marie until ready to serve. At the last minute, swirl in the remaining butter.

SERVES 6

OMELETTE HONGROISE
(*Hungarian Omelette*)

Onion, tomato, and, of course, paprika constitute the filling for this vividly flavored omelette. Excellent for brunches.

10 tablespoons butter
1 medium onion, peeled and chopped
½ cup seeded, drained, and chopped canned Italian tomatoes
Salt
White pepper
Paprika
1 dozen eggs
1 recipe Sauce Hongroise (see above)

1. Heat 2 tablespoons of the butter in each of two small skillets. When the foam subsides, sauté the onion until softened but not browned in one skillet, and the tomatoes, until heated through, in the other. (This can also be done in one skillet—onion first, then tomatoes —but two skillets make the work, if not the washing up, go faster.)

2. Drain away excess liquid from onion and tomato. Combine them in a mixing bowl. Season with salt, white pepper, and paprika.

3. Beat the eggs and season them in preparation for making 6 2-egg omelettes (page 57).

4. Divide the onion-tomato mixture into 6 equal portions of about 2 tablespoons each. Use these portions to fill the omelettes as you cook them with the remaining butter. Surround each omelette with a circle of Sauce Hongroise.

SERVES 6

SAUCE POULETTE

An intensified version of allemande used for vegetables and poached sweetbreads and brains. Escoffier particularly recommends it as an accompaniment for sheep's feet. I have been neither inclined nor able to taste this combination, but I can absolutely vouch for Sauce Poulette with mussels.

1/4 cup mushroom cooking liquid (page 209)
1 cup Sauce Allemande (page 104)
1/3 cup mussel cooking liquid (see below; use only in conjunction with mussel dishes and otherwise omit)
A few drops lemon juice
1 1/2 tablespoons butter
1 teaspoon chopped parsley

1. Reduce the mushroom liquid by two-thirds in a heavy, non-aluminum saucepan.

2. Stir in the Sauce Allemande. Bring to a boil, reduce heat and simmer for 3 minutes. If you are using this sauce with mussels, add their reduced cooking liquid at this point. If the mussels are not finished cooking yet, hold the sauce in a bain-marie until you are ready to add the mussel liquid. Then, when it is ready, add the mussel liquid, return the sauce to the stove, and reduce to desired thickness, stirring.

3. If you are serving this with nonmussel dishes, hold in a bain-marie until ready to use. If it is accompanying mussels, which will already be cooked, proceed directly to finishing the sauce by adding lemon juice, swirling in the butter, and sprinkling on the parsley.

SERVES 6

MOULES A LA POULETTE
(*Mussels à la Poulette*)

Moules Marinière is a big, easy, relaxed, and messy dish. Moules à la Poulette refines the same happy idea into a neat and elegant first course or light summer entrée. Instead of a humble broth and a gargantuan pile of shells, you get mussels on the half-shell enrobed in Sauce Poulette.

6 quarts mussels, prepared à la marinière (page 151)
1 recipe Sauce Poulette (see above)
Chopped parsley

1. Remove the mussels from their cooking liquid as soon as they have opened. Remove and discard 1 half-shell from each mussel. Discard any mussels that either have not opened or are full of sand.

2. Strain ⅔ cup of the cooking liquid and add it to the Sauce Poulette, as indicated above.

3. Arrange the mussels on dinner plates. Pour the sauce over them and sprinkle them with parsley.

Serve immediately.

SERVES 6

✥ SAUCE PRINTANIERE
(SPRING SAUCE)

Beurre Vert à la Printanière (green butter) is the distillation of all that is fresh and green in spinach. The process, which is little known, is the most extreme example I know of the French penchant for purification. You start with a bag of spinach and are left with 2 tablespoons of the greenest, finest purée imaginable, vert d'épinard (green of spinach). This is blended with butter, which is then swirled into an allemande sauce that subsequently turns green as springtime.

Serve with eggs and chicken.

1 cup Sauce Allemande (page 104)
2 tablespoons Beurre Vert à la Printanière (page 194)

1. Bring the sauce to a boil. Hold in a bain-marie until ready to use.

2. At the last minute, swirl in the butter.

SERVES 6

OEUFS A LA PRINTANIERE
(Eggs with Spring Vegetables)

Poached eggs on a bed of peas and carrots with a rich, green sauce. An unusual and striking first course.

1 cup fresh or frozen peas, simmered until tender in lightly salted water and drained
1 cup peeled and diced carrots, sautéed until tender in 2 tablespoons butter
6 thin slices white bread, toasted and with crusts removed
1 dozen poached eggs (page 59)
Salt
Pepper
1 recipe Sauce Printanière (see above)

1. Make sure that peas, carrots, toast, and eggs are all ready to serve at the same time. Peas, carrots, and toast can be held in a warming oven while you reheat the eggs.

2. Arrange toast slices on 6 dinner plates.

3. Mix peas and carrots together gingerly. Season with salt and pepper.

4. Arrange the vegetable mixture in equal amounts on the pieces of toast. Put 2 eggs on each vegetable layer. Pour sauce over the eggs.

SERVES 6

❧ SAUCE RAVIGOTE

There is another sauce called ravigote (a variation on vinaigrette, page 213), which is probably better known than this mixture of velouté, white wine, vinegar, shallot butter, and mixed, chopped herbs. But I think this ravigote deserves its name more than the other. The verb *"ravigoter"* means perk up, invigorate.

Serve it with chicken, brains, and sweetbreads.

¼ cup dry white wine
¼ cup white-wine vinegar
1 cup ordinary velouté (page 102)
2 tablespoons Shallot Butter (page 192)
½ teaspoon each chopped fresh chervil, tarragon, and chive (see Note)

1. Combine the white wine and the vinegar in a heavy, nonaluminum saucepan. Reduce by half.

2. Add the velouté, bring to a boil, reduce heat and simmer for 3 minutes, stirring. Hold in a bain-marie until ready to use.

3. Just before serving, swirl in the Shallot Butter.

Remove from heat and sprinkle on the herbs.

SERVES 6

N O T E : If fresh herbs are unavailable, substitute ¼ teaspoon of the missing herb(s) in dried form. The result will be inferior, and it is probably a better idea, if, as is likely, you can find fresh tarragon and chive but not fresh chervil, to eliminate the chervil and proceed with ¾ teaspoon each of chopped fresh tarragon and chive. Your own frozen herbs will do nicely here.

CERVELLES A LA RAVIGOTE
(*Brains à la Ravigote*)

Delicate brains, surrounded by a ring of puffed duchesse potatoes, with an herb sauce.

1½ pounds calf's brains, soaked, trimmed, blanched, drained, and sliced (page 42)
1 recipe duchesse potatoes piped around the edge of an ovenproof serving dish and browned under the broiler (see page 88)
1 recipe Sauce Ravigote (see above)

1. Blanch the brains until they are fully cooked, about 20 minutes. Do this at about the time you intend to brown the potatoes so that both will be hot and ready to serve at the same time.

2. Arrange the sliced brains inside the potato ring. Pour sauce over the brains.

SERVES 6

Sauces Derived from Chicken Velouté

Chicken Velouté
PAGE 122

Suprême
PAGE 123

Albuféra
PAGE 125

Ivoire
PAGE 126

❧ FOND BLANC DE VOLAILLE ET VELOUTE DE VOLAILLE
(CHICKEN STOCK AND CHICKEN VELOUTE)

There is almost no difference between classic chicken stock (and chicken velouté) and classic ordinary white stock (and ordinary velouté). The methods are exactly the same, except that for chicken stock and chicken velouté you will add 1 stewing chicken of at least 3 pounds (cut into 12 pieces) and 3 additional pounds of chicken backs, necks, and bones to the recipe for ordinary white stock and ordinary velouté (page 102). This obviously gives more chicken flavor to the sauce, which is what you want for the small sauces that follow in this section.

Even so, there are not very many of them, and you may think it is excessive to prepare 5 quarts of very rich chicken stock or velouté at a time. You are the best judge of that. I can only say that I have a constant need for chicken stock in every kind of recipe imaginable. It is a staple. On the other hand, ordinary velouté is more versatile and is the base for a greater variety of sauces, and you could reasonably substitute it for true chicken velouté.

Furthermore, because of the large expense involved in preparing chicken stock by the classic method, I do not want to insist that you use this precious broth in all cooking operations where "chicken stock" is called for. By all means, use a less lavish homemade stock for poaching a whole chicken. Even canned commercial chicken stock is acceptable, but do not try to use it for the sauces. It will not reduce without turning too salty.

SAUCE SUPREME

All the other sauces in this section derive from this one. It is a chicken velouté carried to the highest point of perfection, with stock, mushroom liquid, and heavy cream. You could, of course, make up a large batch of suprême and freeze it, but you would not save much time, and you would be locking up a large amount of chicken stock in one fairly specific sauce.

Serve with eggs, chicken, sweetbreads, and vegetables.

1 cup chicken velouté (see above)
1 cup chicken stock (see above)
1 tablespoon mushroom cooking liquid (page 209)
3 tablespoons heavy cream
1 tablespoon unsalted butter

1. Stir together the velouté, stock, and mushroom liquid in a heavy, nonaluminum saucepan. Reduce by one-third, stirring constantly. During this reduction, pour in 2 tablespoons of the heavy cream little by little. You should end up with a touch less than 2 cups.

2. Strain through a chinois. Finish with remaining cream, off heat. Swirl in the butter.

This will give you enough for two small sauces. If you want to prepare only enough for one meal for 6 people, simply halve the ingredients.

RIS DE VEAU NANTUA
(*Sweetbreads Nantua*)

Nantua, the name of a town in the east of France, is a code word signaling the presence of crayfish. Since crayfish are not readily available in this country outside Louisiana, most of us have to substitute shrimp. This is too bad, but life is an imperfect business.

In this recipe, the crayfish/shrimp are a garnish for whole, braised sweetbreads, a food of supernal texture.

2½ pounds sweetbreads
Juice of ½ lemon
Salt
Butter
½ cup diced salt pork
2 large carrots, peeled and sliced in thin rounds
1 large onion, peeled and thinly sliced
Pepper
1 bay leaf tied in a bouquet with 4 parsley stems and 1 sprig fresh
*   thyme (or dusted with ¼ teaspoon dried thyme)*
1 cup chicken stock, homemade (page 122) or canned
6 large, unpeeled shrimp (or crayfish), simmered in lightly salted
*   water for 5 minutes*
1 cup Sauce Suprême (see above)

1. Place the sweetbreads in a nonaluminum pot. Cover them with cold water. Add lemon juice and 1 teaspoon salt. Set over high heat and stir gently with a wooden spoon until the water begins to boil. At the first sign of boiling, run the sweetbreads under a gentle stream of cold water and drain.

2. Pull away the outer membrane from the sweetbreads. Also cut away the tube that connects the two lobes, if it is present. Arrange the trimmed sweetbreads in a single layer on a clean dish towel. Cover with another towel. Put a board over the towel and weight it with several cookbooks. Let stand several hours.

3. When you are ready to prepare dinner, preheat the oven to 350 degrees.

4. Smear the bottom of an ovenproof casserole with butter. Scatter the salt pork, carrots, and onion over the butter. Season with salt and pepper. Add bay leaf bouquet. Set the sweetbreads on top of the vegetables.

5. Cover the casserole and place over medium heat for 5 minutes.

6. Moisten the sweetbreads with the chicken stock. Bring to a boil, cover, and braise in the oven for 35 to 45 minutes. Baste frequently.

7. Arrange the sweetbreads on a serving platter. (Strain, degrease, and reserve the braising liquid for future use.) Garnish with shrimp (or crayfish). Pour the sauce over the sweetbreads.

SERVES 6

✿ SAUCE ALBUFERA

This is an invention of the Napoleonic era named after Maréchal Suchet, who was made Duc d'Albuféra in 1812. Lake Albuféra is near Valencia in Spain, where Suchet was prominent in the Peninsular Campaign. The culinary appellation occurs first in Carême (as completed by Plumerey) and was possibly inspired by the "Spanish" nature of Pimento Butter.

Serve with poached or braised chicken and duck or with sweetbreads.

1 cup Sauce Suprême (page 123)
2½ tablespoons glace de viande blonde (page 102, step 8), dissolved in 1 tablespoon boiling water
1 tablespoon Pimento Butter (page 194)

Combine all ingredients in a nonaluminum saucepan. Heat to serving temperature. Reduce to desired consistency if too thin. Hold in a bain-marie until ready to use.

SERVES 6

SUPREMES DE VOLAILLE ALBUFERA
(*Chicken Breasts Albuféra*)

This is a radical simplification of a dish that originally called for suprêmes stuffed with chicken forcemeat and was garnished with tartlets containing chicken quenelles, mushroom caps, cockscombs, and truffles.

Butter for the wax paper
3 large chicken breasts, boned and split
Juice of ½ lemon
Salt
White pepper
6 tablespoons butter
1 recipe Sauce Albuféra (see above)

1. Preheat oven to 400 degrees.
2. Butter one side of a round of wax paper cut to fit the inside of a large skillet.
3. Sprinkle the suprêmes (the split chicken breasts) with lemon juice and season with salt and pepper.
4. Heat the 6 tablespoons of butter in the skillet until the foam subsides. Add the suprêmes and spoon butter over them. Cover the chicken with the wax paper, butter side down. Put the skillet in the oven and cook for 8 to 10 minutes. The chicken is done when the flesh is white and springy.
5. Set the breasts on a serving platter. Pour sauce over them. Rice is the ideal accompaniment for this dish.

SERVES 6

SAUCE IVOIRE
(IVORY SAUCE)

The name is almost self-explanatory. It is a Sauce Suprême enriched with glace de viande blonde. Serve it with eggs, chicken, and sweetbreads.

1 cup Sauce Suprême (page 123)
2½ tablespoons glace de viande blonde (page 102, step 8), dissolved in 1 tablespoon boiling water

Combine the 2 ingredients in a nonaluminum saucepan and heat to serving temperature. Hold in a bain-marie until ready to use.

SERVES 6

POULARDE A L'IVOIRE
(*Chicken à l'Ivoire*)

Poached chicken served with a glistening Ivory Sauce and garnished with sautéed cucumbers in heavy cream.

1 4½- to 5-pound chicken or capon
5 to 6 cups chicken stock, homemade (page 122) or canned
1 recipe Sauce Ivoire (see above)
3 medium cucumbers, peeled, sliced in half, and seeded
Salt
2 tablespoons butter
¾ cup heavy cream

1. Poach the chicken in the stock (page 108, steps 2 and 4; disregard references to godiveau and trussing).
2. While the chicken poaches, prepare the cucumbers as follows: Sprinkle with salt and allow to drain for 15 minutes in a colander. Cut into ½-inch chunks (or, to be very special, cut into the shape of small olives). Heat the butter in a skillet until the foam subsides, and then sauté the cucumber over medium heat, covered, for 6 minutes, stirring occasionally. Add the cream and continue cooking, uncovered, over high heat, until the cream has reduced to a thick sauce. Stir occasionally.
3. Drain chicken, set on a serving platter, and coat with some of the Sauce Ivoire. Pass the rest separately.

SERVES 6

Sauces Derived from Fish Fumet and Velouté

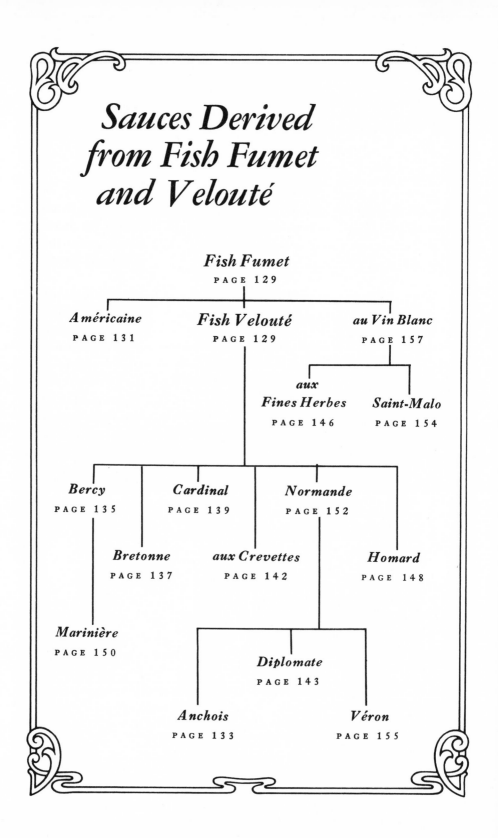

Fish Fumet
PAGE 129

Américaine
PAGE 131

Fish Velouté
PAGE 129

au Vin Blanc
PAGE 157

aux Fines Herbes
PAGE 146

Saint-Malo
PAGE 154

Bercy
PAGE 135

Cardinal
PAGE 139

Normande
PAGE 152

Bretonne
PAGE 137

aux Crevettes
PAGE 142

Homard
PAGE 148

Marinière
PAGE 150

Diplomate
PAGE 143

Anchois
PAGE 133

Véron
PAGE 155

✺ VELOUTE DE POISSON
(FISH VELOUTE)

The basic fish sauce—velouté de poisson—is so rapidly made, in comparison with demi-glace or even ordinary velouté, that there is no overwhelming reason to prepare it in bulk. You must weigh the disadvantage of dealing with several pounds of fish trimmings against the disadvantage of putting in 2 to 3 hours each time you want to get started on one of the classic, flourbound fish sauces.

The recipe for fish fumet (stock) and velouté given here presumes that you would rather opt for efficiency and produce 5 quarts in almost the same time that it takes to produce 1 cup. Freeze the sauce in small containers as usual. If you do not think you will need 20 cups of fish velouté in the ensuing few months, cut the recipe in half. Or quarter it, etc.

Furthermore, since many of the small sauces and dishes mentioned below require fumet as well as velouté, it is probably a good idea to start out by freezing half the fumet you make and converting the rest to velouté. Or, if it suits your purpose and your freezing space better, make velouté in advance and whip up the fumet you need (in 90 minutes, of which only about 30 involve your presence) on the day you need it.

12 pounds fish heads and bones, preferably from sole, flounder, or whiting
1/4 pound (1 stick or 8 tablespoons) butter
3 medium onions, peeled and chopped
3 medium carrots, peeled and chopped
1/2 bunch parsley
2 bay leaves
Stems from 1 pound mushrooms, wiped clean
Juice of 1/2 lemon
1 bottle dry white wine
1 1/2 teaspoons salt
1 tablespoon whole white peppercorns
22 tablespoons (2 3/4 sticks) unsalted butter for roux
3 1/3 cups sifted flour

1. Put the fish trimmings in the sink and soak them in several changes of cold water for 30 minutes.

2. Drain the fish trimmings and chop them roughly with a cleaver or heavy knife.

3. Heat the butter in a large skillet until the foam subsides. Then add the onions and carrots and sauté until softened but not browned.

4. Transfer onions and carrots to a large, nonaluminum pot (if you have one, a lobster pot would be ideal) along with fish trimmings. Stir over high heat for 3 to 4 minutes. Add 5 quarts cold water and all remaining ingredients except white peppercorns, butter for roux, and flour. Bring to a boil, reduce heat and simmer for 20 minutes. Skim occasionally.

5. Add peppercorns. Simmer for another 10 minutes, skimming.

6. Strain through a chinois. You should have about 5½ quarts of fumet. Do not reduce or flavor will be lost. Freeze any fumet you want to store.

7. If you are going to turn all the fumet into velouté, make a blonde roux with the full amounts of butter and flour listed above. Heat the butter in a heavy skillet until the foam subsides. Stir in flour all at once with a wooden spatula or spoon. Blend well. Reduce heat to medium low and cook the roux until it has turned straw yellow. Stir periodically to prevent burning. This may take more or less than 30 minutes, depending on the thickness of the pan, the level of heat, and the diameter of the pan. The roux is done when it has uniformly colored and does not taste raw.

8. Let the roux cool to room temperature.

9. Bring the fumet to a boil in a covered, nonaluminum pot. Let the temperature fall just below a boil, then whisk in the roux. Eliminate any lumps with the whisk and return to the boil. Reduce heat and simmer for exactly 20 minutes. Skim during this time.

10. Let the velouté cool to room temperature, then strain and refrigerate it. Remove the layer of fat that solidifies at the top, and reheat enough to liquefy the sauce. Strain it through a chinois and freeze it in 1- or 2-cup containers.

MAKES ABOUT 5 QUARTS (20 CUPS)

❧ SAUCE AMERICAINE

This is, of course, really a recipe for Lobster à l'Américaine (and can be used, as is, to produce that dish for, say, 2 people), but it becomes a sauce when the entire, finished result is used to complete a yet more complicated seafood preparation. The example of this given below— Filets de Sole à l'Américaine—uses the liquid portion of Lobster à l'Américaine as a sauce, and the solid part—the cooked lobster meat— as a garnish for sole fillets poached in fumet.

There is no question that this is an elaborate way to go about things, but the end result is delicious and it allows you to make a little lobster go a long way.

It is probably unnecessary to add that American sauce is entirely un-American. The name may be a corruption of the old-fashioned adjective for Breton, *armoricain.*

Finally, yes, it is essential to kill the lobster with a knife. Boiling cooks the lobster too definitively to permit the rest of the américaine process to be done without toughening the meat. At any rate, no method of killing lobster is very nice for the lobster. A knife, at least, is quick.

1 2-pound lobster
4 tablespoons oil
10 tablespoons butter
2 large shallots, peeled and chopped
1 small clove garlic, peeled and crushed with the flat of a knife
*   blade*
2½ tablespoons Cognac
¾ cup dry white wine
9 tablespoons fish fumet (page 129)
1 tablespoon glace de viande blonde (page 102, step 8)
3 canned Italian tomatoes, drained, seeded, and chopped
3 tablespoons demi-glace (page 31)
Pinch of cayenne
Parsley, roughly chopped

1. Preheat oven to 350 degrees.
2. With a large chopping knife, slice the lobster in half, length-

wise. It is now dead even if it may still produce some reflex motion for a few moments. Remove the sac near the head and discard. Cut the claws, legs, and tail from the body of the lobster. Crack the claws partially with a nutcracker. Slice the tail, crosswise, into sections at each joint. Remove the coral from the body pieces and reserve in a bowl.

3. Heat the oil and 3 tablespoons of the butter in a large, heavy skillet for which you have a cover. When the oil and butter are very hot but not smoking, put in the lobster pieces and sauté them until the flesh has solidified and the shells have turned bright red. Turn the pieces so that they cook evenly on all sides.

4. When the lobsters are done, hold the lid over the skillet and pour off as much oil and butter as you can. Then sprinkle the lobster pieces with the shallots and garlic. Pour in the cognac and heat it until it vaporizes. Then ignite it.

5. Let the cognac flame, off heat; when the flames have died away, add the white wine, fumet, glace de viande, tomatoes, demi-glace, and cayenne.

6. Set the skillet over high heat and bring the liquid to a boil. Cover the skillet and set in the oven to cook for 20 minutes.

7. Remove the lobster pieces with a skimmer or slotted spoon, letting as much liquid as possible drain back into the skillet. Remove the flesh from the tail sections and the claws. Reserve, along with the other pieces (on two dinner plates in a warming oven, if you intend to eat the "sauce" as is). Discard the tail and claw shells.

8. Reduce the lobster cooking liquid in the skillet to about ¾ cup. While it boils down, pound the coral and 2 tablespoons of butter into a smooth paste. Add this lobster butter to the reduced liquid in the skillet. Blend the sauce with a whisk and strain through a chinois. (If your lobster came minus coral, simply strain the reduced cooking liquid and proceed.) Hold the sauce in a bain-marie until ready to serve.

9. Finish the sauce, off heat, by whisking in the rest of the butter in small pieces. Sprinkle with parsley. (Pour the sauce over the lobster pieces if you are stopping here to eat.)

SERVES 6, AS A SAUCE, OR 2, AS A FISH COURSE

FILETS DE SOLE A L'AMERICAINE

1 recipe Sauce Américaine (see above)
*6 sole fillets, folded over to form triangles and poached in fumet
(page 152, steps 7 and 8)*

1. Having prepared the sauce, reheat the lobster meat in it while the sole finishes poaching.

2. Remove the finished fillets, without unfolding, to a serving platter and arrange them in a circle. (Reserve the poaching liquid, strained, for future use.)

3. Strain the sauce into a sauceboat and fill the center of the circle of sole fillets with the lobster meat. Decorate the platter further with the lobster body pieces and legs.

SERVES 6

❧ SAUCE ANCHOIS
(ANCHOVY SAUCE)

People who don't like anchovies have probably been eating them right out of the can. These savory little fish should be washed thoroughly in order to get rid of their excessive saltiness. Then they are fit to enliven even an elegant Sauce Normande and to accompany all manner of other fish.

1 recipe Sauce Normande (page 152), not finished with butter
1 small (2-ounce) can flat anchovies, washed and wiped dry
2 tablespoons butter, softened

1. While you are preparing the Sauce Normande, chop about ⅓ of the anchovies so finely that they become a paste. Work this into the butter to produce a homogeneous mixture. Push the anchovy butter through a fine strainer.

2. Dice the rest of the anchovies.

3. Hold the sauce in a bain-marie until ready to use. At the last moment, swirl in the anchovy butter and sprinkle on the diced anchovies.

SERVES 6

COTELETTES DE SAUMON A L'ITALIENNE
(*Salmon Cutlets à l'Italienne*)

It was the fantasy of older chefs to cut salmon fillets so that they would look like little chops. They would then cook them and decorate the end cut to look like the tip of the rib bone with a frilled paper sleeve. Nothing prevents you from reverting to this whimsical artifice, but the real interest of this superb recipe is that it yields up a perfectly cooked, juicy slice of salmon (sculpted and frilled or not) coated with mushrooms and then a layer of bread crumbs and Parmesan cheese. Deep frying seals in the freshness of the salmon. The combination of tastes is magnificent. And the cooking is done practically in seconds. Matched with Sauce Anchois (see above), this makes a most elegant and forceful main course.

6 6- to 8-ounce salmon fillets
1½ pounds mushrooms, wiped clean and roughly chopped
3 egg yolks
⅔ cup bread crumbs, approximately
⅓ cup grated Parmesan cheese
Oil for deep frying
1 recipe Sauce Anchois (see above)

1. Cut away all skin from the fillets.
2. Purée the mushrooms in a blender, handful by handful. Add a little water each time to get the process started. Collect each batch of puréed mushrooms in a bowl. When they have all been through the blender, squeeze the purée in a dish towel to extract as much liquid as possible. (Reserve the water for flavoring soups and sauces.) Then put the mushroom solid left in the towel in a bowl. Beat an egg yolk into the mushroom purée to lighten it.
3. Spread the mushroom mixture in a thin layer over one side of each salmon fillet.

4. Mix together the bread crumbs and cheese in a bowl.

5. Beat remaining 2 egg yolks and paint all the salmon fillets on both sides. Then dredge them in the bread-crumb–cheese mixture. Shake off excess and set the breaded "cutlets" on wax paper. Lay a second sheet of wax paper over them and press down lightly on each one.

6. A few minutes before you are ready to eat, heat oil for deep frying. When the oil begins to smoke, fry the cutlets one at a time until golden brown. Drain on paper toweling and keep warm until all are done.

7. As soon as the last cutlet is done, serve. Pass Sauce Anchois separately.

SERVES 6

≈☊ SAUCE BERCY

Bercy is a fundamental, universal fish sauce: sautéed shallots in a reduction of white wine and fumet. Adding fish velouté makes it thick and opaque and grand. A lighter, more impromptu approach eliminates the velouté: The fish is poached in a mixture of half wine and half fumet with shallots. After cooking, the fish is removed and the poaching sauce quickly reduced. At this point, of course, velouté may still be added. How much to add is a question of taste and experience. Options like these are what make the life of the *saucier* interesting. Whichever method you choose, you will still have a Bercy to serve.

2 teaspoons finely chopped shallots
3 tablespoons butter
⅓ cup dry white wine
⅓ cup fish fumet (page 129)
1 cup fish velouté (page 129)
1 teaspoon chopped parsley

1. Sauté the shallots in 2 tablespoons of the butter in a skillet until softened but not browned.

2. Add white wine and fumet. Reduce by one-third as rapidly as possible. The large surface area provided by the skillet makes quick re-

duction almost inevitable. And this is important, because fish fumet loses flavor easily during prolonged cooking.

3. Add fish velouté, bring to a boil, and let bubble for a few seconds. Then remove from heat, swirl in remaining butter, and sprinkle with parsley.

SERVES 6

HUITRES BERCY
(*Oysters Bercy*)

Shucking oysters yourself is hard work, but it is worth it. You spend less money, you get all the delicious oyster liquor, the oysters are fresher, and guests are always surprised to see oysters on the half-shell in a private home. Baked oysters are an even more unusual sight outside of restaurants. Oysters Bercy—poached oysters put back in the shell and covered with sauce, which is then browned under the broiler—produce a dramatic effect indeed.

To shuck oysters efficiently and safely, be sure you use an oyster knife and cover your work area with newspaper to catch the drips. With most American oysters, you will have the best luck if you begin the job by working the point of the knife into the hinge of the oyster, where the two halves join. When the blade goes all the way in, run it around the shell. Then pull the oyster open, remove the meat in one piece, and there you are. This gets easier after the first dozen.

2 dozen unshucked oysters
1 recipe Sauce Bercy (see above)

1. Shuck the oysters. Reserve as much oyster liquor as you can in a large skillet. Also reserve one half-shell from each oyster. The half-shells you keep should be the deeper, more capacious ones. Wash out their insides.

2. Preheat broiler.

3. Bring the oyster liquor to a boil, add oysters, reduce heat and poach (the liquid should not simmer but just quiver slightly) until the edges of the oysters begin to curl.

4. Remove oysters from liquor with a slotted spoon. When they

have drained for a moment, put them into the half-shells. Strain liquor and use a small amount to flavor the sauce and to lighten it, if necessary.

5. Pour about 1 tablespoon of sauce over each oyster.

6. Arrange the oysters in an ovenproof pan or pans. Run them under the broiler close to the heat source; remove as soon as the sauce has browned slightly. Serve 4 oysters to each person. Even 2 of these richly caparisoned oysters will make an adequate first course.

SERVES 6 OR 12

❧ SAUCE BRETONNE

A versatile sauce recommended for eggs, fish, white veal, chicken, sweetbreads, and brains. When used with braised fish, bretonne begins as a cooking liquid composed of white wine and fumet with the julienne strips of leek, celery, onion, and mushroom. After cooking, reduce the liquid and finish with velouté, cream, butter (and salt, if necessary), as indicated below.

3 tablespoons butter
1 tablespoon fine julienne strips (1½ inches long, 1/16 inch wide)
    cut from the white part of a well-washed leek
1 tablespoon fine julienne strips cut from the white part of a rib
    of celery
1 tablespoon fine julienne strips cut from an onion
1 tablespoon fine julienne strips cut from mushroom caps
1 cup fish velouté (page 129)
2 tablespoons heavy cream
Salt

1. Heat 2 tablespoons of the butter in a small skillet until the foam subsides. Add leek, celery, and onion strips and cook slowly over medium-low heat until the strips have softened but not browned. Add the mushroom strips. Stir them together with the other vegetables for a minute or two. Then add all the vegetables to the velouté in a non-aluminum saucepan.

2. Bring the sauce to a boil, reduce heat and simmer for a few minutes, stirring. Hold the sauce in a bain-marie until ready to use.

3. Finish sauce off heat by whisking in heavy cream and remaining butter. Add salt if necessary.

SERVES 6

COTELETTES DE SAUMON POJARSKI
(*Salmon Cutlets Pojarski*)

Here is another way of making factitious cutlets from salmon (for another, see page 134). This time, you chop the salmon and combine it with butter and milk-soaked bread crumbs. The resulting *appareil* is then formed into cutlets and sautéed. If you take the trouble to shape these patties so that they look like real cutlets, you can complete the illusion by putting little frilled paper sleeves over the "bone."

1½ pounds boned, fresh salmon
¼ pound butter, cut into small pieces
1 cup bread crumbs
2 cups milk, approximately
Salt
Pepper
Nutmeg
¼ pound butter, clarified (page 31, step 11)
1 recipe Sauce Bretonne (see above)

1. Cut away the skin from the salmon and discard. Use a thin knife. Scrape the flesh away from the skin and trim off white connective tissue.

2. Chop the salmon roughly. Continue chopping and add the butter as you work. Stop chopping when you have a fairly smooth but not pasty mixture.

3. Immerse the bread crumbs in milk. Then squeeze out excess milk and add the bread crumbs to the salmon mixture.

4. Work the salmon mixture with your hands until it is smooth and homogeneous. Then blend in salt, pepper, and nutmeg to taste.

5. Divide the salmon mixture into 6 parts. Form each one into a flat patty on wax paper.

6. Heat the clarified butter in a large skillet until it is hot, but not so hot that it begins to turn brown.

7. Sauté the salmon cutlets in the butter until they have browned on both sides. Arrange the finished cutlets on a serving platter.

Serve Sauce Bretonne separately.

SERVES 6

❦ SAUCE CARDINAL

Like the red birds called cardinals, this fish velouté tinted pink with lobster coral is named after the red robes and hats of the cardinals of the Church.

Although it may seem disrespectful to connect lobsters with ecclesiastical princes, the association is not limited to the culinary sphere. In French ecclesiastical slang, a cardinal is known as a lobster. For example, when the chauffeur of a French cardinal was once asked why he was loitering by his limo, he is supposed to have replied: *"J'attends mon homard."* ("I'm waiting for my lobster.")

I am also waiting for my lobster. And when he arrives, I hope he will be served with a good Sauce Cardinal. The combination is . . . heavenly . . . a red eminence . . . divine.

Sauce Cardinal is also appropriate for fleshy, white fish, for crabmeat, and for eggs, but it has most often been combined with lobster, since no one has probably ever been profligate enough to throw away a lobster after taking its coral for a sauce.

1 cup fish velouté (page 129)
½ cup fish fumet (page 129)
2 tablespoons coral from a cooked lobster
2 tablespoons butter, softened
½ cup heavy cream
Cayenne
4 teaspoons truffles, chopped (optional)

1. Stir together the velouté and fumet in a heavy, nonaluminum saucepan. Bring to a boil and reduce by half over high heat, stirring often.

2. While the reduction takes place, pound the coral (the soft, red roe of the lobster) and the butter together until well blended. Then push through a fine strainer to make lobster butter.

3. Add the heavy cream to the reduced sauce, return to the boil, and cook for another minute. Hold the sauce in a bain-marie until ready to use.

4. Finish the sauce by swirling in the lobster butter. Also season carefully with cayenne, and add the chopped truffle, if you are using it. Do not use truffle if the dish with which you are serving the sauce already contains truffle.

SERVES 6

COQUILLES DE HOMARD CARDINAL
(*Lobster Coquilles Cardinal*)

The word "coquille" is a cognate of our word cockle. In French it means "shell," as in snail shell or clam shell. A *"coquillage"* is a collection of shellfish. But coquille has also come to refer to one particular shellfish, the coquille St.-Jacques, or scallop. And so it is that a coquille of lobster is a "scallopized" lobster prepared in a style normally reserved for scallops and then presented in scallop shells.

The lobster is first cooked in a court-bouillon, or flavored broth, then diced, and then mixed with Sauce Cardinal. This mixture is set in scallop shells bordered with dauphine potatoes and run under the broiler. Everything can be done ahead except for this final glazing.

2 cups vinegar
4 tablespoons salt
3 pounds carrots, peeled and chopped
2 pounds onions, peeled and chopped
2 sprigs fresh or ½ teaspoon dried thyme

2 bay leaves
1 bunch parsley
4 tablespoons black peppercorns
4 1-pound lobsters
½ recipe appareil dauphine (see page 87)
1 recipe Sauce Cardinal (see above)

1. Combine vinegar, salt, carrots, onions, thyme, bay leaves, parsley, and peppercorns in a large, nonaluminum pot with enough water to cover the lobsters. Bring to a boil, reduce heat and simmer for 1 hour. Let cool so that flavors may intensify. Then strain through a chinois into another pot. If that is a nonaluminum pot, use it for cooking the lobsters. Otherwise, clean the original pot and pour the strained court-bouillon into it.

2. Bring the court-bouillon to a boil. Plunge the lobsters into it, reduce heat and simmer slowly for 15 to 20 minutes. Lobsters are done when they have turned bright red and their antennae pull out easily. Drain the lobsters and let them cool. Strain the court-bouillon and freeze it for future use. When you want to use it again, reboil after adding water to make up for evaporation during previous use.

3. Prepare the *appareil* dauphine. Pipe it through a pastry bag fitted with a star tube to make borders around 6 scallop shells or 6 small, shallow ovenproof dishes.

4. Preheat the broiler.

5. Crack open the lobsters and remove the meat. Cut 6 ¼-inch slices from the tails and reserve. Dice the rest of the meat and mix it together with half the Sauce Cardinal to make what is called a salpicon: diced, solid ingredients held together by sauce and used to stuff something else or in a salad.

6. Fill the scallop shells or dishes with equal amounts of the salpicon. Place 1 of the reserved slices of tail meat on top of each mound of salpicon. If you are using truffle, set a slice on top of each slice of tail meat.

7. Cover the truffle-lobster-salpicon mound with a layer of sauce. Do not cover the potato border.

8. Run the coquilles under the broiler 3 inches from the heat source. When the top layer of sauce has browned lightly, put each coquille on a dinner plate and serve immediately.

SERVES 6

ᰥ SAUCE AUX CREVETTES
(SHRIMP SAUCE)

Here once again is the standard classic fish sauce idea—fumet, fish velouté, and cream—individuated with shrimp butter and pieces of diced shrimp. You will find other recipes that pursue a flashier color effect by adding tomato paste. But the essential shrimp sauce is as follows. Serve it with all manner of fish and shellfish.

1¼ cups fish velouté (page 129)
¼ cup heavy cream
¼ cup fish fumet (page 129) or strained poaching liquid from
*   Filets de Sole à la Trouvillaise (see below)*
4 cooked, unshelled shrimp (see below)
1½ tablespoons butter, melted
Cayenne

1. Stir together fish velouté, heavy cream, and fumet or poaching liquid in a nonaluminum saucepan and reduce to 1¼ cups. Hold in a bain-marie until ready to use.

2. Meanwhile, shell and devein the shrimp. Dice the shrimp and chop the shells. Then combine half the diced shrimp and all the chopped shell in the blender. Pour in the melted butter and purée. (Reserve the remaining diced shrimp.)

3. Push the blended shrimp butter through a fine strainer. Swirl it into the sauce at the last moment. Season cautiously with cayenne. Sprinkle on the reserved diced shrimp.

SERVES 6

FILETS DE SOLE A LA TROUVILLAISE

Trouville is a resort town on the Norman coast of the English Channel, where sole is the preeminent local fish. Sole in the manner of Trouville is poached in fumet, garnished with shrimp and mussels, and napped with shrimp sauce.

2 pounds sole fillets, poached in fumet (page 129)
2 dozen mussels, scraped clean and thoroughly rinsed
1 cup dry white wine
1 tablespoon salt
¼ pound unshelled shrimp
1 recipe Sauce aux Crevettes (see above)

1. At the same time that the sole is poaching, bring 3 cups of water to a boil, and put the mussels in another pot with the white wine. Cover the mussel pot and cook over medium heat until the shells open. Then remove the mussels from their shells, trim them, and keep them warm in their cooking liquid.

2. When the water boils, add the salt and the shrimp. Reduce heat and simmer for about 5 minutes or until shrimp just turn opaque. Drain the shrimp in a colander, reserve 4 of them for making Sauce aux Crevettes, and peel and devein the rest. Add the finished shrimp to the mussels and keep warm.

3. Arrange the sole fillets on a serving platter. Surround them with shrimp and mussels. Pour the sauce over sole, shrimp, and mussels. Serve immediately.

SERVES 6

SAUCE DIPLOMATE

Sauce Normande (page 152) is the mother sauce for a small family of very sophisticated fish sauces, of which Diplomate is probably the grandest, with its superadditions of lobster butter, lobster meat, and truffles. With or without truffles, it is a luxurious affair and would seem to deserve its alternative name, Sauce Riche. Nevertheless, rich though it may be, the sauce is really so called because it was developed at the renowned and long defunct Café Riche in Paris, where it was used with sole. It will go equally well with other delicate fish and with fish quenelles.

2 teaspoons unsalted butter, softened
1 tablespoon coral from a cooked lobster
1 recipe Sauce Normande (page 152)
1½ teaspoons diced, cooked lobster meat
1 teaspoon diced truffles (optional)

1. Pound the butter with the coral in a mortar. Push through a fine strainer.

2. Hold Sauce Normande in a bain-marie until ready to use. Then swirl in the lobster butter and sprinkle on the diced lobster and truffle. If you are not using truffles, you might want to compensate by doubling the quantity of diced lobster.

SERVES 6

QUENELLES DE BROCHET A LA LYONNAISE
(Pike Dumplings à la Lyonnaise)

In Lyon, they make these delicate dumplings from pike. If you can get some, by all means use it. But halibut and flounder are not desperate substitutes for pike. Rather, they are convenient and excellent alternatives.

The trick with quenelles is to end up with a mixture that is light but not so light that it will fall apart in the poaching liquid. Be careful when you add the cream. The quantity given is an approximate amount. In any case, this is the only hard part of this famously "difficult" maneuver. I am preserving the old-fashioned terminology of "panade" and "farce," but it may help to remember that the first is really an unsweetened cream-puff dough finished in minutes and that the second is nothing more than fish ground up fine and mixed with panade, butter, eggs, and flavorings.

FOR THE PANADE
1 cup milk
2 tablespoons butter
1 cup less 2 tablespoons sifted flour
1 whole egg
1 pinch salt

FOR THE FARCE

11 ounces halibut or flounder fillets
The panade (see above)
14 tablespoons butter, melted
4 whole eggs
3 egg whites
6 tablespoons heavy cream, chilled
Salt
White pepper
Nutmeg

FOR COOKING THE QUENELLES

The farce (see above)
Flour
Salt
6 cups fish fumet, approximately (page 129)

1 recipe Sauce Diplomate (see above)

PANADE

1. Pour the milk into a medium saucepan. Add the butter cut into small pieces. Bring to a boil and add the flour all at once. Stir vigorously so as to produce a smooth dough. Remove from heat.

2. Beat in the egg and salt. Then return to the stove and stir over low heat to dry out the dough (and to reduce it to the correct weight, which is ½ pound).

FARCE

1. Put the fish through a food mill or a meat grinder fitted with its finest blade. Repeat the process two more times. You should end up with 1¼ cups fish.

2. Put the ground fish in a large bowl. Knead it until very smooth.

3. Push the panade through a fine strainer and beat it into the fish.

4. Beat the melted butter into the farce (the fish-panade mixture), but be careful to leave the milk solids in the pan as you pour the butter.

5. Next, gradually beat in the eggs and the egg whites.

6. Finally, beat in the heavy cream and season to taste with salt, white pepper, and nutmeg.

7. Chill the farce overnight or until quite stiff. Seal the bowl with plastic wrap.

COOKING

1. Take about ⅒ of the farce and roll it with your hands on a lightly floured board, shaping it into a cylinder 4 inches long. Make 9 more cylinders with the rest of the farce. Set them between sheets of wax paper on a cookie sheet and refrigerate.

2. Bring 4 inches of lightly salted water to a boil in a fish poacher or other pan. Reduce heat so that the water barely quivers, slip the quenelles into the water, and poach for 15 minutes or until the quenelles have solidified. After 10 minutes, shake the pan so that the quenelles roll over (or turn them gently with a spoon). Preheat oven to 350 degrees while the quenelles are cooking (unless you plan to freeze the quenelles when they finish poaching).

3. Drain the quenelles with a slotted spoon and allow them to dry out and solidify further on a dish towel. Then, either freeze them or proceed to the final stage of cooking.

4. Bring 2 inches of fish fumet to a boil in a poacher or other pan. Remove from heat. Slip the quenelles into the fumet. Set the pan on the middle level of the oven. Cook for 10 minutes or until the quenelles have swelled noticeably.

5. Drain the quenelles and put them on a serving platter. Pour on the sauce and serve immediately. (Strain the fumet and reserve for future use.)

SERVES 6 TO 10

SAUCE AUX FINES HERBES
(WHITE WINE HERB SAUCE)

Not to be confused with the brown sauce of the same name (page 70), this is a complex descendant of Sauce au Vin Blanc (page 157) that will suit fish of substantial flavor, especially mackerel and bluefish. As usual, compensate for absent chervil with an equivalent amount of tarragon. The shallot butter is worth making in quantity, since it makes an excellent fish "sauce" in its own right. In fact, it is difficult to think of any nonsweet food that would not be improved with a little shallot butter.

1 recipe Sauce au Vin Blanc (page 157)
4 teaspoons Shallot Butter (page 192)
1 teaspoon chopped parsley
1 teaspoon chopped fresh or ½ teaspoon dried chervil
1 teaspoon chopped fresh or ½ teaspoon dried tarragon

1. The Sauce au Vin Blanc should be held in a bain-marie until ready to use.

2. Swirl in the shallot butter; then sprinkle on the herbs. Stir them into the sauce and let them steep for a minute or two before serving.

SERVES 6 TO 8

MAQUEREAU AU COURT-BOUILLON
(*Mackerel in Court-bouillon*)

A court-bouillon is a flavored liquid, usually water, used to poach fish. It can be frozen and used again after the addition of more water to make up for liquid lost during previous use. The method below is applicable to almost all large pieces of fleshy fish. It adds flavor and yields up tenderness. Once you have made your court-bouillon, nothing could be simpler.

1¼ cups vinegar
1 carrot, peeled and diced
2 sprigs fresh or ½ teaspoon dried thyme
1 tablespoon salt
1 bay leaf
2 onions, peeled and chopped
3 pounds mackerel, cut into ¾-inch steaks
1 recipe Sauce aux Fines Herbes (see above)
Chopped parsley (optional)

1. Add vinegar, carrot, thyme, salt, bay leaf, and onion to 4 quarts of cold water. Bring to a boil, reduce heat and simmer for 1 hour, uncovered. Let cool. Strain.

2. Pour the court-bouillon into a fish poacher. Arrange the mackerel steaks on the rack of the poacher and lower into the cold court-bouillon.

3. Set the poacher over medium heat and let come to a boil. Then reduce heat and simmer slowly for about 25 minutes or until the flesh is opaque, no blood is visible, and a fork penetrates easily.

4. Raise the rack and let the steaks drain. Then transfer them to a serving platter and nap with Sauce aux Fines Herbes. Or serve sauce separately and sprinkle the fish with chopped parsley.

SERVES 6 TO 8

SAUCE HOMARD
(LOBSTER SAUCE)

Another approach to lobster sauce, based on fish velouté and cream. Two compound butters supply personality and color. Use with all delicate fish and, of course, lobster.

1 cup fish velouté (page 129)
¼ cup heavy cream
2 teaspoons unsalted butter
1 tablespoon coral from a cooked lobster
2 teaspoons Paprika Butter (page 193)

1. Hold the fish velouté, enriched with the heavy cream, in a bain-marie until ready to use.

2. Meanwhile, make a lobster butter with the butter and the coral (page 144, step 1).

3. Swirl the lobster and paprika butters into the sauce at the last minute and serve.

SERVES 6

BAR BRAISE, SAUCE HOMARD
(Braised Striped Bass with Lobster Sauce)

Striped bass is one of America's finest large fish. But any big, fleshy, white fish will benefit from braising. Fishermen and people with cooperative fishmongers should also make every effort to clean fish intended for braising through the gills rather than slitting open the bellies, because this helps greatly to seal in the juices and flavor of the fish—the goal of braising in the first place. Clearly, this applies only to fish cooked whole, with the head on.

Braised fish are often covered with buttered wax paper during cooking. Frequent basting is also effective in keeping the whole fish moist.

1 3½-pound striped bass, scaled and cleaned, preferably through
    the gills and a small hole in the abdomen
1 teaspoon chopped parsley
6 tablespoons butter, approximately
Salt
Pepper
1 cup diced carrots
1 cup diced onions
3 parsley stems
1 bay leaf
1 sprig fresh or ¼ teaspoon dried thyme
¾ cup fish fumet (page 129)
¾ cup dry white wine
1 recipe Sauce Homard (see above)
1 tablespoon cooked and diced lobster meat (optional)

1. Run cold water through fish cavity to rinse clean. Then make several slashes with a knife in the fleshy part of the back to a depth of about ½ inch.

2. Work the parsley into 2 tablespoons of the butter; then work in a small amount of salt and pepper. Push this butter into the fish's cavity through the hole in the abdomen (or spread it over the cavity of a con-

ventionally cleaned fish). Sprinkle the outside of the fish with salt and pepper.

3. Preheat oven to 325 degrees.

4. Heat 3 tablespoons butter in a skillet until the foam subsides and sauté carrot and onion until softened but not browned.

5. Spread the carrot and onion across the rack in a fish poacher. Add parsley stems, bay leaf, and thyme to this vegetable bed. Then set the bass into the poacher. Pour fumet and white wine over it. Bring to a boil over medium heat, then transfer to the middle level of the oven. Cover the fish with buttered wax paper.

6. Cook for 45 minutes or until a fork penetrates the fish easily. Baste frequently.

7. Raise the rack and drain the fish. Transfer to a serving platter. Pass Sauce Homard (garnished with the diced lobster meat, if you wish) separately.

The braising liquid can be strained and used as a sauce in its own right. If it is too thin, reduce and/or thicken with cream or butter.

SERVES 6

🦞 SAUCE MARINIERE

This is an egg-bound variation of Sauce Bercy specially flavored with the cooking liquid from Moules Marinière. The idea is elaborate, but the preparation is not. And the rewards are twofold: a magnificent sauce and an inexpensive meal. Mussels are one of the last remaining seafood bargains.

Marinière can also be served with white, fleshy fish.

1 recipe Sauce Bercy (page 135), minus parsley
¼ cup strained cooking liquid from Moules Marinière (see below)
2 egg yolks, lightly beaten and at room temperature

1. Hold the Sauce Bercy in a bain-marie while the mussels cook.

2. Reduce cooking liquid to 1 tablespoon and stir into the sauce.

3. Whisk egg yolks into the sauce. Cook over medium heat until the yolks have thickened. Do not boil.

SERVES 6

MOULES, SAUCE MARINIERE
(*Mussels, Marinière Sauce*)

Mussels steamed in white wine—Moules Marinière—are a great treat served in the shell, in great piles, with the broth in the same bowl. But mussels cooked in the same rapid manner can also be served neatly on the half-shell with a grand sauce flavored with their essence.

6 quarts fresh mussels
½ cup finely chopped shallots, scallions, or onions
10 parsley stems
2 cups dry white wine
1 bay leaf
1 teaspoon fresh or ¼ teaspoon dried thyme
White pepper
8 tablespoons (1 stick or ¼ pound) butter
1 recipe Sauce Marinière (see above)
2 tablespoons chopped parsley

1. Scrub the mussels clean with a wire brush or steel wool. Pull away the "beard" that seems to grow out of the opening between the two shells. Discard any mussels that are either open or markedly heavier or lighter than the norm. Soak the rest in cold water for 2 hours.

2. In a 10-quart pot, combine shallots (or scallions or onions), parsley stems, white wine, bay leaf, thyme, white pepper, and butter (cut into small pieces). Bring to a boil and cook for 3 minutes.

3. Add mussels, cover, and cook over medium-high heat for 5 minutes, stirring the mussels once after 3 minutes. When the mussels have opened, they are done.

4. Remove and discard 1 shell from each mussel. Arrange the mussels on the half-shell on dinner plates and keep hot in warm oven. Simultaneously, you should be reducing the strained cooking liquid for the sauce.

5. Finish the sauce and pour it over each mussel. Sprinkle with parsley and serve immediately.

Excess cooking liquid can be strained and reserved for future use in sauces or in cooking mussels.

SERVES 6

ꙮ SAUCE NORMANDE

Normandy cream is justly famous; thick and rich, it is the basis, along with Normandy butter and apples and seafood, of a great regional cuisine. Sauce Normande in the version below is the classic, that is to say national, version of a somewhat different regional sauce. Basically, it is a reduction of fish fumet, velouté, and heavy cream. Serve it with sole, other delicate fish, and oysters.

1 cup fish fumet (page 129), or strained poaching liquid from
*   Filets de Sole à la Normande (see below)*
3 tablespoons finely chopped mushroom stems
1 cup fish velouté (page 129)
½ cup plus 5 tablespoons heavy cream
4 tablespoons unsalted butter
Salt

1. Combine the fumet or poaching liquid with chopped mushroom stems in a nonaluminum saucepan and reduce by half.
2. Add fish velouté and ½ cup of the cream. Reduce by half, stirring.
3. Off heat, whisk in the remaining heavy cream, the butter, and a little salt, if necessary. Strain through a chinois.

SERVES 6

FILETS DE SOLE A LA NORMANDE

Sole Normande prepared in the classic manner (see description below) is a tableau of garnishes which I can see no reason to re-create at home. Various suggestions for simplifying the dish are given in the recipe. It would really be enough to poach the sole in fumet and serve it with the sauce, but the dish, in its full-blown antique version, is so renowned that it would also be sacrilege, or at least a mistake, not to delineate what it once is supposed to have been. You must decide how far you want to insist on historical accuracy.

Butter
1 tablespoon finely chopped shallots
2 parsley stems
1 sprig fresh or ¼ teaspoon dried thyme
1 bay leaf
6 mussels, cleaned, debearded, and soaked for 2 hours
1 cup dry white wine
Salt
6 mushroom caps
6 unpeeled shrimp
6 unshucked oysters
2 pounds sole fillets
1 recipe Sauce Normande (see above)
6 truffle slices (optional)
6 small lozenges of white bread fried in butter (optional)

1. Butter the bottom of a small skillet. Sprinkle the chopped shallots over the butter. Add the parsley stems, thyme, bay leaf, and mussels. Scatter 2 tablespoons of butter cut into small pieces over the mussels. Add ½ cup of the white wine, cover, and cook for a few minutes over high heat until the mussels open. Shuck the mussels and reserve in a covered pot in a warming oven. Strain the cooking liquid and reserve.

2. In a small, nonaluminum saucepan, combine the rest of the wine, 1 tablespoon butter, and salt. Bring to a boil and add mushroom caps. Simmer for 5 minutes. Drain mushroom caps and keep warm along with mussels. Reserve the cooking liquid.

3. Bring 2 cups water to a boil. Pour in 1 tablespoon salt. Then plunge the shrimp into the water, reduce heat and simmer for 5 minutes or until shrimp turn opaque. Drain, peel, and devein the shrimp. Keep warm with mussels. Discard cooking liquid.

4. Shuck the oysters and collect their liquor in a small saucepan (directions for shucking are on page 136). Bring the liquor to a boil, lower heat, add oysters, and poach in barely quivering liquid until the edges of the oysters begin to curl. Drain the oysters, trim them, and keep them warm with the mussels. Reserve cooking liquid.

5. Preheat oven to 375 degrees. If you have been keeping the cooked garnishes warm in that oven until now, remove the saucepan containing them from the oven and set it, covered, in hot water.

6. Butter a baking dish large enough to hold the sole fillets in an overlapping layer. Put in the fillets.

7. Stir together the reserved cooking liquids from the mussels, mushrooms, and oysters. Pour this liquid over the sole until the liquid level comes about halfway up the sole. If there is not enough liquid, compensate with cold water (or fish fumet, page 129).

8. Bring the liquid to a boil, cover the fish with a piece of buttered wax paper, and set in the oven for 8 to 12 minutes, until fish is white and firm but not flaky. Drain gently.

9. Arrange the fillets on individual plates. Arrange the mussels, mushrooms, shrimp, and oysters around them. Pour sauce over the sole and the garnishes.

If you wish to garnish the dish in something like the classic manner, put a truffle slice and a bread lozenge on each sole portion.

Formally speaking, Sole Normande called for 3 truffle slices on each side of each fillet, alternating with 6 bread lozenges. Surrounding this were crayfish and fried gudgeons. Perhaps an American cook could substitute smelt for gudgeons (*goujons* or *Gobio gobio*). But this dish seems quite baroque enough to me without piling on rare garnishes. Even Escoffier wrote that truffles were optional in this recipe.

SERVES 6

❧ SAUCE SAINT-MALO

Brittany begins at Saint-Malo, which is also an old pirate stronghold. Perhaps the spirit of the buccaneers is preserved in this piquant offspring of Sauce au Vin Blanc. The special ingredients are shallot butter, mustard, and anchovy paste. Serve it with broiled fish.

1 cup Sauce au Vin Blanc (page 157)
2 tablespoons Shallot Butter (page 192)
2 teaspoons Dijon mustard
Anchovy paste

1. Hold the Sauce au Vin Blanc in a bain-marie until ready to use.

2. Just before serving, swirl in the shallot butter. Then whisk in the mustard and a smidgeon of anchovy paste.

SERVES 6

BROILED RED SNAPPER SAINT-MALO

*2 2-pound (or 1 4-pound) red snappers, cleaned but with heads
    and tails intact*
Salt
Pepper
Oil
3 tablespoons butter
6 small potatoes, boiled, peeled, cooled, and cut into rounds
Parsley
Lemon wedges
1 recipe Sauce Saint-Malo

1. Preheat broiler.

2. Season fish inside and out with salt and pepper. Slash the fleshy
part of the back in several places to a depth of about ½ inch. Paint the
fish with oil.

3. Oil a sheet of aluminum foil and set it on the broiler tray. Put
the fish on the foil and run it under the broiler, as far as possible from
the heat source. Broil about 4 minutes on each side or until flesh is white
and a fork penetrates it easily.

4. While the fish is broiling, heat the butter in a skillet with 2
tablespoons of oil. Put in the potato rounds and fry until crisp.

5. Place fish on a serving platter and arrange the potatoes around
the sides of the platter. Put parsley at either end of the platter. Serve
lemon wedges and sauce separately.

SERVES 6

❦ SAUCE VERON

To commemorate the nineteenth-century gastronome Dr. Véron
(page 12), we combine two sauces and jus de veau for a very *raffiné*
result.

½ recipe unsalted Sauce Normande (page 152)
¼ cup Sauce Tyrolienne (page 177)
4 teaspoons unthickened jus de veau (page 35)
½ teaspoon anchovy paste, approximately

1. Hold the Normande in a bain-marie.
2. Whisk the Tyrolienne into the Normande.
3. Reduce the jus de veau by half and stir into the sauce.
4. Whisk in the anchovy paste and serve.

The sauce may begin to separate at the table, but it can be easily stirred back together.

SERVES 6

FILETS DE BARBUE VERON
(*Flounder Fillets Véron*)

2 pounds flounder fillets
Salt
Pepper
Flour
1 whole egg at room temperature
1 teaspoon oil
1 cup bread crumbs, approximately
1 recipe Sauce Véron (see above)

1. Preheat broiler.
2. Season fillets with salt and pepper.
3. Put a handful of flour on a sheet of wax paper.
4. In a small bowl, whisk together egg, oil, ½ teaspoon salt, and pepper. Blend well.
5. Dredge the fillets in the flour and shake off excess. Then paint the fish sparingly with the egg-oil mixture. Dredge in bread crumbs. Shake off excess and press fillets lightly between two sheets of wax paper.

6. Lay a sheet of lightly oiled aluminum foil on the broiler tray. Put the flounder on it and run under the broiler 3 inches from the heat source. Cook about 2 minutes on each side.

7. Transfer fillets to a serving dish and pour sauce over them.

SERVES 6

❧ SAUCE AU VIN BLANC
(WHITE WINE SAUCE)

Really a fish hollandaise, Sauce au Vin Blanc is also a little mother sauce (see chart, page 128). If you wonder when you look at the recipe where the white wine comes in, remember that you used some to make the fumet. Its acidity, especially after the reduction for this sauce, is what promotes the emulsification of the butter and egg yolks.

¼ cup fish fumet (page 129)
2 egg yolks, lightly beaten
13 tablespoons unsalted butter, melted and then cooled, but still
    pourable
Salt

1. Reduce fumet by half in a nonaluminum skillet. Transfer to a clean, heavy, nonaluminum saucepan.

2. Now proceed as if you were making hollandaise (page 171). Whisk the egg yolks into the reduced fumet, and continue whisking over very low heat until the egg yolks thicken. The heat of the fumet may be sufficient to bring this about immediately, even before you put the saucepan over low heat.

3. As soon as the yolks have thickened, start whisking in the butter. Add only a drop or two at first, then pour in a fuller stream as the sauce begins to take. Whisk constantly.

4. When you have incorporated all the butter, add salt to taste. Then strain through a chinois and serve immediately.

SERVES 6

SOUFFLE DE HOMARD
(*Lobster Soufflé*)

A first course for very special friends—because of the cost, not the labor. Soufflés are much easier than they look. And you can ease the financial jolt of serving lobster by using frozen lobster meat, which is cheaper than its equivalent in live lobsters. Since, moreover, the meat is ground up for a soufflé, you will not be compromising in any appreciable way; the texture of the lobster itself is not an issue here.

Butter
12 ounces (about 2 cups) cooked lobster meat
3/4 cup Sauce Béchamel (page 161)
Milk (if necessary), scalded
4 egg yolks, lightly beaten
Salt
White pepper
4 egg whites
1 recipe Sauce au Vin Blanc (see above)

1. Preheat oven to 400 degrees.
2. Butter the inside of a 4-cup soufflé dish or charlotte mold. Butter the inside of a paper collar and tie it onto the soufflé dish so that it comes 2 inches above the top of the dish.
3. Put the lobster through the fine blade of a meat grinder.
4. Mix together the lobster and the béchamel in a bowl. If the béchamel is too thick to pour, loosen it with a small amount of scalded milk.
5. Stir the egg yolks into the lobster mixture. Season with salt and white pepper.
6. Beat the egg whites until they are stiff but not dry.
7. Stir 1/4 of the beaten egg whites into the lobster mixture. Fold in the rest.
8. Turn the soufflé mixture into the buttered dish. Smooth off the top, gently. Set the dish in the middle level of the oven. Turn heat down to 375 degrees immediately and bake for about 30 minutes. The soufflé is done when it has risen and browned on top.

Serve Sauce au Vin Blanc separately.   SERVES 4

The
Béchamel
Family

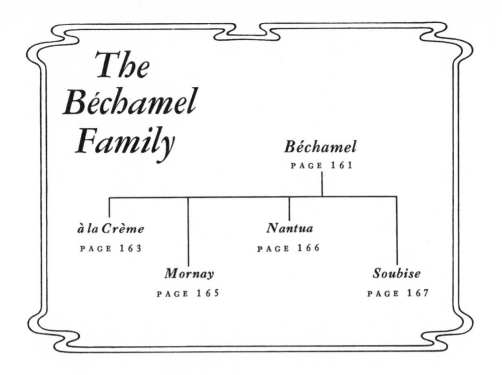

The Béchamel Family

Béchamel
PAGE 161

à la Crème
PAGE 163

Nantua
PAGE 166

Mornay
PAGE 165

Soubise
PAGE 167

SAUCE BECHAMEL

Gastronomic literature is filled with tedious passages and trifling disputes. Béchamel has inspired more than its fair share of this piffle. People *will* argue about whether it was invented by the Marquis Louis de Béchameil; whether the correct spelling should not be béchamelle; whether the Italian version, balsamella from the Romagna district, is the original of this best-known and easiest mother sauce.

In such matters prejudice will always rule, for there is no evidence one way or the other. We can only point to the appearance of a sauce called béchamel during the reign of Louis XIV. And, as so often, this original sauce bore only a slight resemblance to the modern sauce. While we think of béchamel as an all-purpose white sauce made of scalded milk, roux, and flavorings, Carême made it by enriching velouté with cream.

The modern sauce is also in dispute. Recently, a distinguished popular historian wrote me a testy note in which she accused me of printing a recipe for "ordinary white sauce" and then jumping it up to the exalted status of béchamel, which, she pontificated, must always contain veal.

The historian was refusing to pay attention to a legitimate variation in culinary practice that goes back a long way. Some chefs, we know from early cookbooks, have always flavored their béchamels with veal; others have not. The difference in taste is minor. Béchamel with veal is, indeed, a slightly more interesting product. But béchamel without veal is not to be snubbed, especially since the basic role of the sauce is neutral and mundane.

It is a vehicle. It thickens and binds and coats. It goes with almost anything, from cauliflower to veal to lasagne. Two versions of the sauce are given below, one with veal, one without. Both are from classic sources. Both can be frozen. Both, please note, are meant to come out very thick. The reason for this is that it is easy to loosen up a béchamel with a little scalded milk or cream, but more difficult to thicken it at the last minute. And you will be wanting béchamels of varying thicknesses for varying purposes. The finished sauce, when ready to use, should always be pourable.

BECHAMEL WITH VEAL

10 tablespoons unsalted butter
1½ cups sifted flour
¼ pound lean veal, diced
1 small onion, peeled and chopped
1 sprig fresh or ¼ teaspoon dried thyme
2 quarts milk
White pepper
Nutmeg
1 teaspoon salt, approximately

1. Melt 8 tablespoons of the butter in a heavy skillet. Heat until the foam subsides.

2. Add flour all at once. Stir it into the butter with a wooden spatula. Continue stirring over medium-low heat until the roux has lost its raw taste. This should not take more than 5 minutes. The roux should not color. When it is cooked, scrape the roux into a bowl and let it cool to room temperature.

3. Meanwhile, heat the remaining butter in a skillet until the foam subsides. Stir in the veal, onion, and thyme. Lower heat to medium, cover, and cook until the onion is transparent. Stir occasionally to prevent browning of onion or meat.

4. Bring milk to a boil in a large, nonaluminum saucepan. When the milk starts to foam, reduce heat and whisk in the roux. Continue whisking until all lumps have disappeared.

5. Add the veal mixture, return to the boil, reduce heat and simmer very slowly for an hour. Stir occasionally.

6. Season to taste with white pepper, nutmeg, and salt. Strain, cool, and freeze in small containers.

MAKES APPROXIMATELY 2 QUARTS

BECHAMEL WITHOUT VEAL

Ingredients are the same as in the first recipe, except that you should eliminate 2 tablespoons of butter and the veal.

1. Prepare the roux as in the first version.

2. Boil the milk in a large, nonaluminum saucepan. When it starts to foam, lower heat, add onion (raw) and other seasonings, and simmer for 10 minutes, covered.

3. Whisk in the roux. Keep whisking until well combined. Simmer, uncovered, for another 15 minutes.

4. Strain, cool, and freeze in small containers.

MAKES APPROXIMATELY 2 QUARTS

❧ SAUCE A LA CREME

This is nothing more than béchamel finished with cream. You can substitute milk, if you wish. The point here is to loosen and enrich the mother sauce so that it can be served.

1½ cups Sauce Béchamel (page 161)
1 cup heavy cream
1 teaspoon lemon juice, approximately
Salt
Pepper
Nutmeg

1. Stir together the béchamel and ¼ cup of the heavy cream in a large, nonaluminum saucepan. Reduce quickly to about ¾ cup, stirring constantly.

2. Strain and hold in a bain-marie.

3. When ready to serve, stir in the remaining heavy cream and the lemon juice, to taste. Add salt, pepper, and nutmeg to adjust final seasoning.

SERVES 6

MORUE A LA CREME
(*Creamed Salt Cod*)

This can be a dish of great purity, if you soak the fish properly. French chefs love to serve it at home, and so will budget-minded Americans.

3 pounds salt cod
1 recipe Sauce à la Crème (see above)

1. Soak the salt cod for 72 hours in plenty of cold water. Change the water twice daily.

2. Boil enough water to cover the cod (which should be spread in a single layer, not piled up), add the cod, bring to a boil again, reduce heat and simmer very slowly for 15 minutes.

3. Remove the cod from the water and drain it thoroughly. Flake it with a fork, discarding any bones or skin. At the same time, heat the sauce.

4. Stir the cod pieces into the sauce and simmer slowly for 10 minutes, stirring.

5. Arrange in a mound on a serving platter. Boiled new potatoes will go nicely with this very rich dish.

SERVES 6

❧ SAUCE MORNAY

Mornay, a béchamel with cheese, is the classic sauce for coating eggs, vegetables, fish, or chicken before they go under the broiler to be glazed. The recipe below is brought back to appropriate thickness with heavy cream. If you are going to use Mornay with fish or chicken, it is better to substitute juices from the chicken or fish being cooked or chicken stock (page 122) or fish fumet (page 129) for the cream.

1 cup Sauce Béchamel (page 161)
1/2 cup grated Gruyère cheese
1/2 cup grated Parmesan cheese
Heavy cream
Up to 4 tablespoons unsalted butter

1. Heat the béchamel until it boils. Reduce heat to low.
2. Stir in the Gruyère and Parmesan so that they melt and blend into the sauce.
3. Loosen the sauce to desired consistency (usually this will mean until it can just be poured) with heavy cream.
4. Swirl in the butter off heat.

SERVES 6

OEUFS CHIMAY
(*Chimay Eggs*)

Stuffed eggs with a yolk-mushroom filling coated with Mornay Sauce, Parmesan cheese, and butter. A lovely first course that can be assembled ahead of time and glazed at the last minute.

1 dozen hard-boiled eggs, shelled and sliced lengthwise into 24 halves
1/2 pound mushrooms, finely chopped and sautéed in 2 tablespoons butter to make about 1 cup duxelles (page 67)
1 recipe Sauce Mornay (see above)
1/2 cup grated Parmesan cheese
4 tablespoons unsalted butter, melted

1. Preheat the broiler.

2. Remove the egg yolks and collect them in a bowl.

3. Drain the duxelles. Squeeze in a dishtowel to extract remaining liquid (which you should save to use for another purpose—in a soup or a sauce). Stir duxelles into the egg yolks and blend to a homogeneous mixture.

4. Stuff the egg halves with the yolk-duxelles mixture. Set them in a shallow, buttered baking dish or individual ramekins.

5. Pour Mornay Sauce over the stuffed eggs. The sauce should be barely thick enough to pour; reduce it if necessary.

6. Sprinkle the Mornay coating with Parmesan. Drizzle butter on top of the cheese.

7. Run the eggs under the broiler at the top level, so as to brown the tops lightly and heat the eggs through.

SERVES 6

✿ SAUCE NANTUA

Nantua, a town in the Jura mountains of eastern France, has given its name to this béchamel, which is flavored (and colored) by crayfish, or, absent crayfish, by shrimp.

Serve with chicken, fish, eggs, and shellfish.

1 cup Sauce Béchamel (page 161)
6 tablespoons heavy cream
¼ cup unshelled crayfish tails or unshelled shrimp, sautéed until
    opaque in 2 tablespoons oil; or ⅓ cup small, bottled Danish
    shrimp, drained
2 tablespoons unsalted butter
Domestic paprika (optional)
5 additional sautéed crayfish tails or shrimp; or 15 small Danish
    shrimp, for a garnish

1. Combine hot béchamel with 4 tablespoons of the heavy cream and reduce over medium heat to 1 cup, stirring constantly.

2. Stir the remaining heavy cream into the sauce off heat.

3. Pound the crayfish tails or shrimp as smooth as possible with the butter (or purée in the blender, melting the butter first). Push through a fine strainer.

4. Add the strained crayfish butter to the hot sauce. Blend well. If you do not get an acceptably pink color, stir in paprika until you do.

5. Hold the sauce in a bain-marie. Two or three minutes before serving, add the shellfish garnish.

SERVES 6

POULARDE NANTUA
(*Chicken Nantua*)

2 3-pound roasting chickens, poached in chicken stock (*page 109, steps 2 and 4; disregard references to godiveau and trussing*)
Parsley
1 recipe Sauce Nantua (see above)

Drain the chickens and set them on a serving platter. Decorate with parsley. Pour the sauce over the chickens. Serve with rice.

SERVES 6

SAUCE SOUBISE

Soubise is an ancient preparation named after a noble house. It is, properly speaking, an onion coulis or purée rather than a sauce, and its primary modern uses are as the most delicious feature of Veal Orloff and as a surprisingly attractive accompaniment to other meat dishes.

1 medium onion, peeled, sliced, and simmered in lightly salted water for 8 to 10 minutes
4 tablespoons butter
1 cup Sauce Béchamel (page 161)
1 pinch sugar
¼ cup heavy cream, approximately

1. Preheat oven to 350 degrees.

2. Drain the onion.

3. Heat 2 tablespoons of the butter in a saucepan until the foam subsides. Add the onion and cook, covered, over medium-low heat until the onion is golden but not browned, about 20 minutes.

4. Heat the béchamel and stir it together with the onion and the sugar. Bring to a boil and place in the middle level of the oven. Cook for another 15 minutes.

5. Strain through a chinois, pressing hard on the onions.

6. When ready to use, reheat the sauce and swirl in the remaining butter. Soubise should be quite thick, but if you want to lighten it a bit, stir in the heavy cream.

SERVES 4

COTES DE VEAU ORLOFF
(*Veal Chops Orloff*)

A streamlined version of a famous dish: veal chops stuffed with Soubise and glazed with Mornay.

4 tablespoons butter
4 thick veal chops
1 recipe Sauce Soubise (see above), reduced almost to a paste
8 truffle slices (optional)
1 recipe Sauce Mornay (page 165)

1. Heat the butter in a large skillet until the foam subsides. Add the veal chops and sauté until browned on both sides and cooked through to desired degree of doneness, about 4 minutes per side.

2. Preheat broiler.

3. Cut a pocket in each chop (page 39).

4. Stuff each pocket with 3 tablespoons of the Soubise. Then insert 2 truffle slices in each chop, if you wish.

5. Arrange the stuffed chops on a sheet of aluminum foil on the broiler tray. Spread a tablespoon of Soubise across the top of each chop. Pour Sauce Mornay over each chop and glaze at the upper level of the broiler until lightly browned on top.

SERVES 4

The Emulsified Sauces

To a chemist, an emulsion is a dispersion of liquid globules in another liquid. This phenomenon is also the basis of several of the finest French sauces: béarnaise, hollandaise, mayonnaise, and their variations. Behind these marvels is the simple fact that an egg yolk will emulsify surprising quantities of oil or butter.

Since the emulsified sauces are all quite fragile and cannot be frozen, there is no way of making them in quantity and keeping them around. You could prepare a large quantity of herb reduction for béarnaise during the tarragon season and freeze it. But that is as close to a mother sauce as this "orphaned" family gets. There are an almost infinite number of possible mayonnaises and hollandaises, but they must all be made from scratch. Therefore, it could be said that the emulsified sauces lie outside the general framework of this book, which is primarily concerned with restaurant-style, quantity batches of freezable sauces. But it was impossible to imagine a handbook of sauces that did not include béarnaise and its cousins. If you already possess recipes for them, the next three chapters will at least give you all of them in one place. I am not, however, offering a recipe for a characteristic dish to go with each of these emulsified sauces, for their use is well known. But I have noted some general suggestions which might not occur to many home cooks.

Hollandaise and Its Cousins

🦞 SAUCE HOLLANDAISE

Almost everything can go wrong with a hollandaise. It can curdle. It can separate. It can be too thick or too loose or too sour. But there are ways to guard against or correct any of these minor catastrophes.

Some people use a blender, which gives a fast, sure—and mediocre —result: Blender hollandaise comes out too thick. Others resort to the double boiler, a dodge I deplore, because it slows everything down and because the hidden water can still boil and wreck the sauce. The cold butter method is also safe—the temperature of the butter helps keep the yolks from scrambling—but it is slow and can create special problems of timing.

The best way to make a quick, sleek hollandaise is the old way, over direct heat with lukewarm, melted butter. You must use a heavy pan and, above all, you must concentrate. But in the end you will have more control over the texture of the finished sauce, which should be firm but light.

Serve hollandaise with poached eggs, vegetables, and fish.

¼ pound (1 stick or 8 tablespoons) unsalted butter
¼ cup white-wine vinegar
½ teaspoon salt, approximately
¼ teaspoon white pepper
2 egg yolks
½ teaspoon lemon juice

1. Melt the butter and allow it to cool partially. It should be warm when used below in step 3.

2. In a heavy, nonaluminum, 1-quart saucepan, stir together the vinegar, salt, and white pepper. Reduce by half, to about 2 tablespoons, and remove from heat. Let cool to room temperature.

3. Whisk the egg yolks into the vinegar reduction. Place the saucepan over very low heat and whisk constantly, until the yolks have turned white and thickened visibly. Remove from heat and immediately begin whisking in the warm butter a drop at a time. As you progress, after the sauce has clearly "taken," you can gradually increase the amount of butter you add until you have incorporated all the butter.

4. Strain the sauce through a warm chinois (run it under hot water just before using) into a warm, clean saucepan.

5. The sauce is now ready to serve. Lighten it, if necessary, with a few drops of cold water. Whisk in the lemon juice (this should always be done at the last minute to avoid souring the sauce). Taste the hollandaise and add more salt or lemon juice if necessary. Serve in a hot, dry sauceboat.

6. If you must hold the sauce, do so in water that is no hotter than 140 degrees, and do not try to extend the wait more than 2 hours. The sauce will evaporate and have to be lightened with cold water.

If butter begins to leak out of the emulsion, which happens when the temperature of the sauce rises above 140, whisk in a little cold water to bring it back. If, on the other hand, the sauce becomes too cool, whisk in a bit of hot water.

SERVES 6

SOUFFLE D'ASPERGES
(*Asparagus Soufflé*)

1 pound frozen asparagus, cooked according to directions on package and drained (*see Note*)
Butter
Grated Parmesan cheese
6 egg yolks
Salt
Pepper
7 egg whites
1 recipe Sauce Hollandaise (*see above*) or Sauce Maltaise (*see
below*)

1. Preheat oven to 325 degrees.
2. Purée the asparagus in a blender or a food mill, then push it
through a chinois and let it cool in a bowl. You should end up with
about 1½ cups of purée.
3. Meanwhile, butter the inside of a 2-quart (8-cup) soufflé dish
or charlotte mold. Then dust the buttered surfaces with Parmesan
cheese. Set aside.
4. Beat the egg yolks into the cooled asparagus purée. When well
blended, season with salt and pepper to taste.
5. Beat the egg whites until stiff but not dry. Stir a small amount
of the whites into the asparagus mixture, to lighten it. Then fold in the
rest of the egg whites.
6. Pour the soufflé mixture into the prepared mold. Smooth off the
top gently. Bake immediately at the lowest level of the oven for approximately 40 minutes. The soufflé is done when it has browned on
top, risen fully, and started to pull away from the sides of the dish.
Serve immediately. Pass sauce separately.
This soufflé will not have a runny center. The batter is too heavy
to cook well at the higher heat required to produce that effect.

SERVES 6

NOTE: It is not worth the trouble to grind up fresh asparagus for this
recipe. If you must, steam 1¼ pounds to account for extra fiber.

VARIATIONS ON HOLLANDAISE

SAUCE AUX CÂPRES (*Caper Sauce*)
Stir 1 tablespoon of drained capers into the master recipe. Serve with any poached fish.

SAUCE MALTAISE (*Maltese Sauce*)
Substitute the juice of ½ orange and 1½ teaspoons grated orange peel for the lemon in the master recipe just before serving. Tradition specifies blood oranges for this sauce. These red-tinted oranges are sometimes available in American markets, and they will give the sauce a more interesting color; however, orange oranges will produce approximately the same effect—lower acidity and a lighter texture than normal hollandaise—with an almost equally appealing color variation. Maltaise is customarily matched up with asparagus.

SAUCE MOUSSELINE (*Muslin Sauce*), also known as
SAUCE CHANTILLY (*Chantilly or Whipped Cream Sauce*)
Add 2 tablespoons of just-stiffened, whipped heavy cream to the master recipe just before serving. Serve with poached fish, asparagus, artichokes, and braised celery.

SAUCE MOUTARDE (*Mustard Sauce*)
Add 1 tablespoon of Dijon mustard to the master recipe just before serving. Serve with broiled fish.

❧ SAUCE BEARNAISE

A relatively new sauce (page 11), béarnaise is now a universal favorite, almost everyone's choice for the greatest of all sauces. Indeed, this sophisticated, thickish combination of a vinegar-shallot-tarragon-chervil reduction, egg yolk, and butter is a wonderful thing, and not a Sisyphean labor, although it cannot be stored. It requires no costly advance preparation—it has no mother—and it is the preeminent sauce for the preeminent contemporary dish: grilled meat. Béarnaise also goes beautifully with grilled fish, especially salmon.

1/3 cup tarragon vinegar
1/2 cup dry white wine
2 tablespoons finely chopped shallots
3 tablespoons fresh chopped or 1 tablespoon dried tarragon
2 tablespoons fresh chopped or 2 teaspoons dried chervil
1/2 teaspoon crushed white peppercorns
3 egg yolks
1/2 pound unsalted butter, melted
Salt
Cayenne

1. In a heavy, nonaluminum skillet, combine the vinegar, wine, shallots, 2 tablespoons of the fresh or 2 teaspoons of the dried tarragon, 4 teaspoons of the fresh or ½ teaspoon of the dried chervil, and the crushed white peppercorns. Bring to a boil and reduce by two-thirds, to slightly more than ¼ cup. Let cool.

2. Whisk the egg yolks into the herb reduction and cook slowly over low heat, whisking constantly. When the mixture acquires a creamy consistency, remove from heat and gradually drizzle the butter into it, whisking as you pour. Strain through a chinois.

3. Plunge the remaining herbs into a tablespoon of boiling water. Let stand for a minute or so. Drain. Then stir into the sauce. Taste the sauce and season with salt and a small amount of cayenne.

"It is useless to imagine," says Escoffier, "that you can serve this sauce, which is basically a mayonnaise with butter, while it is hot. It is sufficient that it be warm. Besides, if it is overheated, it will decompose.

"In that event, you can return it to its normal state by adding a few drops of cold water and working it with a whisk." In other words, you can hold a béarnaise for a while, say one course or a round of drinks, but no longer, without running into problems.

SERVES 6

VARIATIONS ON BEARNAISE

Like béarnaise itself, all these sauces are particularly suited to grilled meat or fish.

SAUCE ARLÉSIENNE

Drain, seed, and chop 1 canned Italian tomato. Stew it for 10 minutes in 1 tablespoon butter. Purée in a food mill and stir into the finished béarnaise sauce along with a small amount of anchovy paste.

SAUCE CHORON

Omit step 3 in the master recipe. Instead of adding the extra herbs, beat 4 teaspoons of tomato paste into 4 teaspoons of heavy cream and stir the mixture into the béarnaise.

SAUCE FOYOT, *also called* SAUCE VALOIS

Omit step 3 in the master recipe. Instead of adding the extra herbs, whisk 3 tablespoons of melted glace de viande (page 30) into the béarnaise. Foyot should be the color of light coffee.

SAUCE PALOISE

Substitute chopped fresh mint leaves for the tarragon in the master recipe.

SAUCE TYROLIENNE

Substitute 1 cup oil for butter in the master recipe. Stir approximately 2 tablespoons tomato paste into the finished sauce. Add the tomato paste gradually and stop when you get a healthy, red color. This goes well with grilled chicken (see below). It is also a component of Sauce Véron (page 155).

POULET GRILLE TYROLIENNE
(*Grilled Chicken Tyrolienne*)

3 2½-pound chickens, halved
6 tablespoons butter
Oil
1½ recipes Sauce Tyrolienne (see above)

1. Prepare a charcoal fire in an outdoor grill with a large enough surface to accommodate the 6 chicken halves. When all the coals are white, the fire is ready.
2. Meanwhile, spread 2 tablespoons of the butter on the insides

of the chicken halves. Push the rest, cut in pieces, under the skin of the thighs and breasts.

3. Begin grilling with the meat side down. Let the fire sear the chicken briefly, then raise the grill 2 or 3 inches higher. Cook in this position for 10 minutes. Paint the chicken with oil frequently.

4. Turn the chicken and lower the grill to sear the other sides. Raise the grill and cook until done, when juices run clear from the thickest part of the thighs. Paint with oil as before.

Pass sauce separately.

SERVES 6 TO 8

An Anatomy of Mayonnaise

◈ MAYONNAISE

Here is a foolproof way to produce enough mayonnaise for 8 serious eaters who want to while away an afternoon with wine and a selection of raw vegetables. It will also suffice for a family of four, used randomly, for a week.

1 egg yolk
1 teaspoon vinegar or lemon juice
Salt
Pepper
1 teaspoon Dijon mustard
1 cup oil, approximately

1. Beat the yolk vigorously with the vinegar or lemon juice, salt, pepper, and Dijon mustard.
2. Begin dribbling oil into the yolk mixture a drop at a time, beating in the oil as you go along. After a time, the mayonnaise will "take," will gain body and turn into a recognizable mayonnaise. Then, you can begin pouring in the oil more rapidly, whisking all the while. Continue

until all the oil has been used up. If the mayonnaise turns (i.e., if it separates or curdles), stir in a small amount of mustard, which will bring it back.

3. Stir a tablespoon or so of boiling water into the finished mayonnaise in order to set it, so that it will not separate. Refrigerate in a clean, tightly sealed jar.

This is all extremely easy, as easy as making mayonnaise in a blender, and the hand method gives you control over the final texture. You can make a stiffer or thinner mayonnaise depending on how much oil you incorporate. Purists will say that true mayonnaise does not use mustard to hold the sauce together. Purists will say anything so long as it makes our life more difficult. Leave the mustard out if you must, but be prepared to exercise much more caution with the sauce and to incorporate only ¾ cup oil, on the average—that is, be prepared to end up with significantly less sauce. I can see no advantage in the taste of a mustardless mayonnaise.

That is all you need to know about mayonnaise, except that it can be varied with most edible materials to produce new sauces. Classic variations are nearly all made by whisking in a tablespoon (or more, according to taste) of additional flavoring or coloring elements to a basic, 1-yolk mayonnaise. Here are a few standards:

Sauce Echalote: Finely chopped shallots added.

Sauce Dijonnaise: Enough extra Dijon mustard added so that the taste emerges distinctly.

Sauce Chantilly: Whipped cream added.

Shrimp Mayonnaise: Pound 1 large, shelled, cooked shrimp to a paste with 2 tablespoons mayonnaise, then sieve and add to sauce. Include the shell when you pound, to add color—if you like.

Sauce Rémoulade: Small amounts of anchovy paste, chopped gherkins, capers, parsley, chervil, and tarragon.

All standard herbs, curry powder, garlic, and even puréed caviar are effective flavorings for mayonnaise.

These mayonnaises go particularly well on a buffet table with cold poached salmon or bass, cold roast beef, and most raw vegetables.

Butter
Sauces

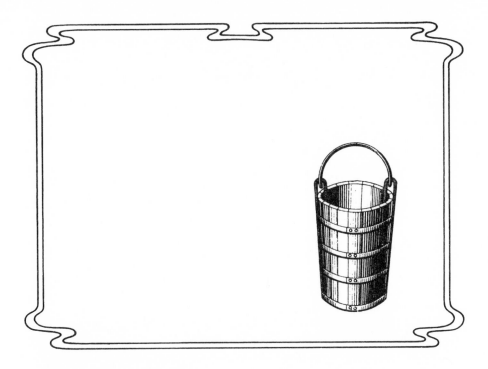

❧ BEURRE BLANC
(WHITE BUTTER)

Beurre blanc is not, strictly speaking, a classic sauce. It is, however, a classic of the regional cuisine of the west of France. And in modern French luxury restaurants, this housewife's specialty has become a spécialité de la maison. It also has a reputation for extreme difficulty. Most recipes tell you that beurre blanc requires a flair or some indescribable knack. The trick, if there is one, actually consists of nothing more than exercising extra care to keep the heat low and remembering to start with well-chilled butter. As you whisk in the butter pat by pat, it lowers the temperature of the sauce and gives you extra control. This makes it a certainty that the emulsion—a highly acid reduction plus a large amount of butter—will hold together and stay silken smooth.

Traditionally, beurre blanc was served with the pike and shad of the Loire. It is also magnificent with poached chicken.

Beurre blanc left to cool will decompose. You *can* hold the hot sauce in a bain-marie, but this is tricky because the water bath should not be warmer than 100 degrees. It is really easier in the long run to make the sauce at the last minute. Leftover sauce should be refrigerated.

When you need it, let it soften at room temperature; then pull it back together with an electric mixer and serve it cold. The heat of the food will melt and warm it.

2 tablespoons finely chopped shallots
¼ teaspoon white pepper
½ teaspoon salt
½ cup white-wine vinegar
¾ to 1½ pounds (3–6 sticks or 24–48 tablespoons) unsalted
  butter, chilled

1. Combine 1 tablespoon of the shallots, white pepper, salt, and vinegar in a small, nonaluminum saucepan. Reduce by three-quarters, to approximately 2 tablespoons. Do not underreduce. The final reduction must be as acid as possible without boiling away altogether.

2. Remove reduction from heat. While it is still hot, strain it into a clean, heavy, nonaluminum 4-cup saucepan.

3. Crush the remaining shallots lightly with the flat of a large knife and add them to the reduction. Set the saucepan over very low heat. Then add 4 pats of butter (about 2 tablespoons) and start whisking.

4. As soon as the first 4 pats of butter have almost melted, add 4 more. Continue in this manner until you have melted in all but one stick of butter. All the while you must whisk and continue to add fresh pats of cold butter as soon as the previously added butter has melted appreciably.

5. Remove from heat and whisk in the remaining stick of butter. Correct seasoning and serve immediately.

Three sticks of butter will give you an ample amount of sauce for 6 to 8 people, but the reduction will absorb the full 1½ pounds if you are having a large dinner. Don't be upset if the sauce is not dazzlingly white. American butter is, for the most part, rarely light enough in color to let you achieve visual success with this sauce, but you should end up with at least a straw-colored triumph of delicate taste.

ALOSE GRILLEE
(*Broiled Shad*)

4 to 5 pound's boned fillets of shad (*or pike, bluefish, or mackerel*)
Salt
Pepper
1/2 cup oil
Juice of 1 lemon
1 bay leaf
4 sprigs parsley
1 tablespoon fresh or 1 teaspoon dried thyme
Lemon wedges
1 recipe Beurre Blanc made with 3/4 pound butter (*see above*)

1. Season the shad with salt and pepper and set it for 1 hour in a marinade consisting of the oil, lemon juice, bay leaf, parsley, and thyme. Turn the shad twice.

2. Preheat broiler.

3. Drain but do not wipe off the shad. Put the broiler tray at its lowest level. Cover with a sheet of aluminum foil. Set fillets on the foil, skin side down, and run under the broiler for about 15 minutes. They will be done when lightly browned on top. Serve on a large platter surrounded with lemon wedges. Pass the sauce separately in a warm sauceboat.

SERVES 8

❧ SAUCE AU BEURRE OR SAUCE BATARDE
(BUTTER OR BASTARD SAUCE)

This is technically a custard sauce. You can make something like it by stirring egg yolks and cream together with the deglazed, reduced pan juices from a roast (about 4 yolks per cup of heavy cream) and heating gently until the sauce thickens. But Bastard Sauce itself is made apart from the food you will serve it with, and has no direct culinary relationship to it or to any other stock or mother; whence the name.

From another perspective, though, Bastard Sauce has a quite legitimate, and respectable, lineage. It derives from the practice of Carême,
who used it as the mother (out of wedlock?) of an entire series of
compound white sauces that later came to be based on allemande.

At any rate, here is a surprisingly elegant and outstandingly easy
sauce, which goes well with asparagus and poached fish.

2½ tablespoons sifted flour
8 tablespoons butter, melted
Salt
1 cup boiling water
2 egg yolks beaten lightly with
    2 teaspoons heavy cream
A few drops lemon juice

1. Beat together the flour and 2 tablespoons of the melted butter
until well blended. Stir a small amount of salt into the boiling water and
then pour it all at once over the flour-butter mixture. Beat vigorously
until well blended. Use a wire whisk for this.

2. Now whisk in the egg yolks and cream. When the mixture is
homogeneous, whisk in the lemon juice. Then push through a chinois.

3. The sauce can be held in a bain-marie until needed. Don't let
the water bath boil or even exceed the temperature of hot tap water.
When you are ready to use the sauce, whisk the remaining melted butter
into it and serve.

SERVES 6

ANGUILLE FRITE A L'ANGLAISE
(*Fried Breaded Eel*)

Eel, contrary to legend and appearance, is neither especially slip-
pery nor shocking to eat. Indeed, in all countries known to me where eels
thrive, except the United States, they are considered a major delicacy. The
ancient Greeks prized the eels of Lake Copaïs in Boeotia. Germans dote
on smoked eels. The Chinese of Peking make a specialty of baby eels
(which crossword puzzle solvers know are technically called "elvers").
The French have also applied their ingenuity to this estimably tender,

sweet fish in countless ways—in stews and pâtés, poached and fried. If you have never tried eel, which is sold in Italian, Chinese, and other immigrant neighborhoods, this recipe is an extremely simple introduction to a foolishly snubbed food.

2½ pounds fresh or frozen eel
1 cup oil
Juice of 1 lemon
Salt
Pepper
1 bay leaf
1 sprig fresh or ¼ teaspoon dried thyme
Oil for deep frying
2 recipes Sauce Anglaise (page 198)
1½ cups bread crumbs, approximately
Anchovy paste
1 recipe Sauce au Beurre (see above)

1. Skin the eel by working the skin loose with a thin knife and pulling it away in strips. Slice the flesh away from the central bone.

2. Cut the boned eel into 3-inch-long strips. Soak these in a marinade made from the oil, lemon juice, salt, pepper, bay leaf, and thyme for 4 hours, unrefrigerated. Stir twice.

3. Drain the eel on paper toweling.

4. Heat the oil for deep frying until it sizzles when a sprig of parsley is dropped into it.

5. Roll the eel pieces in the anglaise. Dredge them in the bread crumbs, shake off excess, and fry in small batches until golden brown. Drain finished batches on paper and keep warm in a very low oven until all the eel is fried.

6. Whisk a small amount of anchovy paste into the sauce. Pass separately, along with the eel.

SERVES 6

Compound Butters

The various beurres composés are combinations of flavoring elements and butter. Cooks of the pre-electric era pounded the ingredients together to a smooth paste and then forced the paste through a hair sieve. This is no longer necessary. A blender and a chinois will do the job beautifully. You simply melt the butter, pour it over the solid ingredient in the blender jar, and whirl away. With very small quantities this will not work well, because the blades of the blender may not reach down far enough in the jar. If this looks likely, you will have to revert to the mortar, but there is not much work to pounding a couple of tablespoons.

With or without blenders, compound butters end up the same: concentrated reservoirs of taste that can be added to sauces—for flavor or color—or used as sauces in their own right. The best-known compound butter used by itself is Beurre Maître d'Hôtel or parsley butter (see below). It goes with anything that parsley goes with. Once you have made it—or any of the compound butters—you can keep it for a day or so in the refrigerator, covered, and slice off a pat for each serving of steak or whatever. Or freeze air-tight. Put the pats on the meat and let them melt into instant sauce. My favorite compound butter is made with equal weights of blanched shallots and butter. Shallot butter is a universal condiment that goes with red meat, fish, or vegetables.

In all the recipes below (except where special directions are given), it is assumed that you will follow this method:

1. Rinse the blender jar in hot water and dry it.
2. Put in the solid ingredient(s).
3. Pour in the butter.
4. Purée.
5. Strain through a chinois, pushing hard on the solid residue.
6. Pour into a dish or mold and refrigerate until solid.

BEURRE CHIVRY or BEURRE RAVIGOTE
(*Chivry or Ravigote Butter*)

> *2 clenched fistfuls of fresh chervil, tarragon, chive, and parsley in whatever proportion to each other is feasible; 1/4 each is ideal*
> *2 tablespoons chopped shallots*
> *1/4 pound butter*

Blanch the herbs and shallots in lightly salted, simmering water for 3 minutes. Drain and press out excess water. Combine with butter as in master recipe above.

See page 114 for application.

BEURRE D'ECHALOTE (*Shallot Butter*)

> *2/3 cup chopped shallots*
> *1/4 pound unsalted butter*

Blanch the shallots for 3 minutes in lightly salted, simmering water. Drain. Combine with butter as in master recipe.

Universally applicable.

BEURRE D'ESTRAGON (*Tarragon Butter*)

> *4 tablespoons fresh tarragon leaves*
> *6 tablespoons unsalted butter*

Blanch the tarragon in lightly salted, simmering water for 3 minutes. Drain. Combine with butter as in master recipe.

Universally applicable.

BEURRE DE HOMARD (*Lobster Butter*)

1 tablespoon coral from a cooked lobster
2 tablespoons unsalted butter, softened

Pound together briefly in a mortar. Push through a fine strainer. (This can also be done with lobster debris, shells and all, in the blender. Chop the debris into small pieces. Using ¼ pound melted butter per ½ cup of chopped debris, blend debris with melted butter briefly. Pour out and reheat. Blend again. Strain and refrigerate.)
See page 148 for application.

BEURRE À LA MAÎTRE D'HÔTEL (*Maître d' Butter*)

2 teaspoons finely chopped parsley
Pepper
Juice of ⅛ lemon
¼ pound butter, softened

Combine all ingredients in a bowl and beat together to blend well. Universally applicable.

BEURRE DE MOUTARDE (*Mustard Butter*)

2 teaspoons Dijon mustard
¼ pound unsalted butter, softened

Beat the mustard into the butter until both are well blended. Use with broiled meats and chicken.

BEURRE DE PAPRIKA (*Paprika Butter*)

1 tablespoon butter for sautéing
2 teaspoons paprika
1 tablespoon finely chopped onion
9½ tablespoons unsalted butter

Sauté the paprika and onion in butter until the onion has softened. Proceed as in master recipe.
See page 148 for application.

BEURRE DE PIMENTOS (*Pimento Butter*)

3 tablespoons (2 ounces) drained, rinsed, and finely chopped
*   pimento*
10 tablespoons unsalted butter

Proceed as in master recipe.
See page 125 for application.

BEURRE VERT À LA PRINTANIÈRE
(*Green Springtime Butter*)

10 ounces (1 package) spinach, washed, drained, and finely
*   chopped*
2 tablespoons unsalted butter, softened

Purée the spinach in a blender with ½ cup water. Empty the purée onto a dishtowel and squeeze as much liquid as you can into a 4-quart saucepan. Discard the solid residue in the towel.

Heat the spinach liquid over simmering water for a few minutes, stirring, until it thickens, that is, until it appears to coagulate as a green, silty mash. Remove from heat. Stretch a clean dishtowel over a mixing bowl and pour the coagulated liquid onto it. Do not squeeze the towel; just let it drain. The green solid that is left on the towel (about 2 tablespoons) is called vert d'épinard. Beat it together with the butter in a clean bowl. Push the green butter through a chinois.

See page 119 for application.

Dessert
Sauces

The French, at home and not on view, frequently finish a meal with a dessert of plain jam or marmalade. For them, the word dessert still carries its root meaning: the course eaten after the table is cleared, *desservi*. And even at special dinners, cheese and/or fruit suffice for this normally informal stage of the meal. This is not to say that French cooks have not displayed their customary genius in an array of elaborate desserts running from soufflés to tarts to sophisticated bombes. Nevertheless, it is the case that dessert in France is a coda rather than an essential dénouement to eating, as it is in other countries, notably Austria. Consequently, or coincidentally, French dessert sauces are few in number and not a major aspect even of the French dessert menu. They are accessories after the fact, adventitious fillips. Often they have been adapted from recipes common everywhere. And yet, in the hands of the great French chefs, such commonplaces as chocolate sauce, custard sauce, and fruit syrup have been refined with a Gallic flair, and they have been firmly attached to the French culinary structure, given specific uses, and, if you will, meanings not found elsewhere. French custard sauce, Crème à l'Anglaise or English custard, is usually flavored with Grand Marnier or another liqueur before it is poured over fresh fruit, fruit tarts, or floating island. Sabayon, the French version of Italian zabaglione, is flavored with French sweet wines or spirits and served, canonically, with puddings, as a sauce, not by itself as in Rome. Chocolate sauce as Escoffier made it is a careful concoction that includes vanilla and cream and butter. And it is now associated almost exclusively with the pear sundae named Poires Belle Hélène, named after the Offenbach operetta.

The majority of French dessert sauces, however, are really nothing more than sieved and heated jams—sugared fruit purées—sometimes flavored with liqueurs. It would be pedantic to include them all here, for they are adumbrations of a single thought, and anyone can invent a dozen of his own from fruits and fruit preserves.

Here, then, are a few special sauces for special occasions paired with desserts they might have accompanied at the finish of a grand meal at the turn of the century.

❧ SAUCE ANGLAISE
(ENGLISH SAUCE)

4 egg yolks
½ cup sugar
¾ cup heavy cream
½ cup milk
2 tablespoons vanilla extract

1. Whisk the yolks and sugar together (or beat with an electric mixer at high speed) until the mixture has turned very pale.

2. Stir in heavy cream and milk.

3. Cook over medium heat in a heavy-bottomed pan, stirring constantly, until the sauce thickens noticeably. This will occur at around 165 degrees on a candy thermometer. At this temperature, the sauce will be too hot to touch comfortably.

4. Strain immediately through a chinois to remove any pieces of scrambled yolk. Stir in vanilla.

NOTE: The sauce can be further flavored with various spirits. The orange liqueurs, particularly Grand Marnier, are in common use. Four tablespoons added at the last minute will suit most palates. This sauce can be made a few hours ahead and refrigerated. It is so easy to prepare that there is no reason to freeze it in quantity.

SERVES 8

PUDDING SOUFFLE GRAND MARNIER

Butter for the molds
7 tablespoons unsalted butter, softened
½ cup sugar
1 cup sifted flour
1¼ cups scalded milk
5 whole eggs, separated
4 tablespoons Grand Marnier
1 recipe Sauce Anglaise flavored with Grand Marnier (see above)

1. Butter 8 ⅔-cup custard molds and set aside.

2. Cream the butter with a wooden spoon, whisk, or electric beater. That is, beat it until it has lightened in color and texture. Then gradually beat the sugar and flour into the butter.

3. When the mixture is smooth, beat in the milk. Bring the mixture to a boil. Stir it over medium heat to dry it out as you would a cream puff dough (page 86, step 5).

4. Remove the mixture from the heat. Stir in the egg yolks and the Grand Marnier.

5. Beat the egg whites until stiff but not dry. Stir ¼ of the whites into the pudding mixture to lighten it. Then fold in the rest of the egg whites.

6. Pour the pudding into the buttered molds, filling them three-quarters full. Set them in a shallow pan of simmering water. Cook until the pudding has set, about 2 hours. Add boiling water as needed. Remove from the water. Let cool. Then, run a knife around the side of each mold, unmold on serving plates, and refrigerate until ready to use.

Serve sauce separately.

MAKES 8 INDIVIDUAL PUDDINGS

❧ SAUCE AU CHOCOLAT

9 ounces sweet chocolate
1 tablespoon sugar
½ teaspoon vanilla extract
3 tablespoons heavy cream
1 tablespoon unsalted butter

1. Break up the chocolate into pieces and set it in a small saucepan with 1⅔ cups water. Bring the water to a boil while stirring the chocolate into it as it melts.

2. When the sauce boils, add sugar and vanilla, lower heat as far as possible, and continue to cook for 25 minutes. Then stir in the cream and butter.

This is best to do just before you need it. Reheating solidified chocolate is almost more trouble than starting the recipe from scratch.

SERVES 8

BAVAROIS RUBANE
(Ribboned Bavarian)

8 egg yolks
1¼ cups sugar
Salt
2 cups milk
1 teaspoon vanilla extract
1½ packages gelatin dissolved in 3 tablespoons of cold water
2 ounces sweet chocolate
2 cups heavy cream, chilled
1 recipe Sauce au Chocolat (see above)

1. Beat together the yolks, sugar, and a pinch of salt until the mixture is smooth and pale.

2. Combine the milk and vanilla in a large saucepan, bring to a boil, and stir into the yolk mixture. Then stir in the dissolved gelatin.

3. Put the mixture from step 2 into a heavy-bottomed saucepan.

Cook over medium heat, stirring constantly until the mixture thickens noticeably. Thickening occurs just above 160 degrees on a candy thermometer, when the mixture will be too hot to touch comfortably.

4. Strain the custard mixture through a chinois to eliminate any scrambled yolk particles. Let cool to room temperature. Pour half the custard into another bowl.

5. Meanwhile, immerse the chocolate in very hot tap water. As soon as the chocolate begins to melt, pour off the water and whisk the chocolate into one of the two bowls of cooling custard.

6. When the custard has cooled, whip the cream until stiff. Fold half of it into one bowl of custard and the rest into the other bowl.

7. Now assemble the pudding in a series of white and chocolate layers. Pour enough of the chocolate custard into a large glass bowl to make a 1-inch layer. Set the bowl in the freezer for a few minutes, just long enough so that the custard begins to set. Then add a white layer. Set it in the freezer until it starts to set. Continue in this way, alternating between white and chocolate, until all your custard has been used up. Be careful to make the "ribbons" as uniform in depth as possible and try to make them neatly horizontal.

8. Chill in the refrigerator, covered with plastic wrap, for several hours or overnight. Serve from the bowl. Pass sauce separately.

SERVES 8

꣠ SAUCE SABAYON

1 cup sugar
6 egg yolks
1 cup dry white wine (or Madeira, sherry, Marsala, Asti, or other
    fortified or sweet wine)
3 tablespoons dark rum or kirsch (optional)

1. Whisk the sugar and egg yolks together (or beat with an electric mixer) until the mixture is smooth and very pale.

2. Stir in the wine.

3. Whisk constantly over low heat in a heavy-bottomed, non-

aluminum pan until thick and foamy. You will get a much better result in a round-bottomed, copper zabaglione pan. Serve immediately.

4. If you use dry white wine, then flavor the sauce, off heat after it is otherwise finished, by whisking in rum or kirsch or any other alcohol you choose. This flavoring is unnecessary if you use a fortified or sweet wine.

SERVES 6

PECHES NINETTE
(*Peaches Ninette*)

6 ripe freestone peaches
2 cups fresh strawberries, with stems and leaves removed
3 tablespoons kirsch
3 tablespoons maraschino
Sugar
1 recipe Sauce Sabayon (see above)

1. Plunge the peaches into boiling water. Remove them immediately with a skimmer and put them into ice water. The skin will now pull away quite easily. Use a knife only when necessary. Peel all the peaches.

2. Cut a small hole at the top of each peach, where the stem was. Take a larding needle (a stiff knitting needle will do) and push it into the bottom of each peach. Keep pushing until the pit emerges from the top. Pit all the peaches.

3. Set the peaches in a large serving bowl. Then arrange the strawberries in the spaces left between them.

4. Sprinkle the fruit with the kirsch and the maraschino. Then dust with sugar. Cover the bowl with plastic wrap and refrigerate until ready to serve. There should be an interval of several hours here, while the fruit macerates. Turn the fruit once or twice during this period.

5. Pour the sauce over the fruit an hour or two before serving. Cover the bowl and chill.

SERVES 6

Fruit Sauces

SAUCE A L'ABRICOT
(APRICOT SAUCE)

1 cup apricot preserve
4 tablespoons sugar
4 tablespoons kirsch, Madeira, maraschino, or dark rum

1. Push the preserve through a chinois into a saucepan. Stir the sugar into it and then add a small amount of water, not more than ½ cup, to loosen up the sauce.

2. Bring to a boil. Continue cooking over high heat until the sauce coats the back of a wooden spoon. This happens between 225 and 228 degrees on a candy thermometer. While the sauce cooks, skim it carefully. You should also be stirring the sauce during the 2 or 3 minutes all this will take.

3. Remove from heat and stir in the alcohol of your choice. Serve while still quite hot. If the sauce is too thick to pour easily, relax it by stirring in hot water until it reaches the desired consistency. This method will also help with a sauce that has cooled and solidified.

SERVES 6

POIRES MARIETTE
(*Pears Mariette*)

6 *ripe pears*
6 *tablespoons lemon juice*
½ *cup sugar*
2 *tablespoons vanilla extract, approximately*
1 *pound canned chestnut purée*
1 *recipe Sauce à l'Abricot with rum* (*see above*)

1. Peel and halve the pears. Cut away the stems and cores. As you finish with each half, put it into 4 cups of water acidulated with 2 tablespoons of lemon juice to prevent discoloration.

2. Bring a quart of water to a boil. Stir in the sugar, the remaining lemon juice, and 1 tablespoon of the vanilla. When the sugar has dissolved, add the pear halves. Lower heat so that the water barely trembles and poach for 8 minutes.

3. Let the pears cool in their syrup. Then drain them on a rack.

4. Meanwhile, beat the vanilla into the chestnut purée. Add additional vanilla if you wish. Then form the purée into a mound on a serving platter.

5. Arrange the pears around and over the chestnut purée. Pour some of the sauce over the pears. Pass the rest of the sauce separately. (If you wish, make a sauce by reducing the pear cooking liquid to 1 cup.)

SERVES 6

SAUCE AUX FRAMBOISES
(RASPBERRY SAUCE)

2 *cups raspberry preserve*
3 *tablespoons kirsch*

Combine the preserve and kirsch in a saucepan. Bring to a boil, stirring with a wooden spoon. Then push through a chinois. Loosen with hot water if necessary.

SERVES 8

PUDDING AU PAIN A LA FRANCAISE
(*French Bread Pudding*)

Butter for the mold
2¼ cups dry bread crumbs
2 cups milk
1 teaspoon vanilla extract
10 tablespoons sugar
2 whole eggs
3 egg yolks, lightly beaten
2 egg whites
1 recipe Sauce aux Framboises (see above)

1. Butter the inside of a 4-cup soufflé dish or charlotte mold. Dust the inside with bread crumbs and set aside.

2. Put the milk into a large saucepan. Stir the vanilla and sugar into it. Bring to a boil; then remove from heat.

3. Stir 2 cups of bread crumbs into the scalded-milk mixture. Let soak briefly. Then push through a chinois into a bowl. Stir the whole eggs and egg yolks into the milk–bread-crumb mixture.

4. Beat egg whites until stiff. Fold into the pudding mixture.

5. Pour the pudding into the buttered mold. Set it into a pan of simmering water which is deep enough to come halfway up the side of the mold. Cook until the pudding is firm, about 3½ hours. The water bath should just barely tremble. Keep up water level with additions of boiling water.

6. Let the pudding cool. Run a knife around it and invert it on a serving platter. Unmold and serve with Sauce aux Framboises on the side.

SERVES 8

Miscellaneous

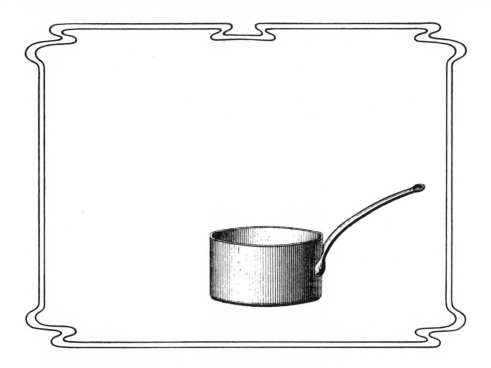

❧ CUISSON DE CHAMPIGNONS
(MUSHROOM COOKING LIQUID)

To produce a mushroom liquid that does not darken, cook ¼ pound sliced mushrooms in ½ cup simmering water that has been lightly salted and acidulated with a few drops of lemon juice for 10 minutes. Drain the mushrooms, which can be used in any dish requiring cooked mushrooms or in a salad. Strain the liquid and store it in a sealed bottle in the refrigerator until needed for Sauce Allemande (page 104) and related sauces.

❧ FOND DE GIBIER
(GAME STOCK)

Since it is unlikely that most hunters will be able to provide the precise ingredients listed below at any one time—and since the combination is not sacrosanct but only an indication of the way to go—feel free to use any of these materials you may have on hand to supplement the ones that are missing, and follow the same basic procedure. You should try to include 5 pounds of meat and bones (of which roughly two-thirds of the total weight should be due to the bones).

1¼ pounds venison trimmings, cubed
¼ pound hare trimmings, cubed
½ mature wild rabbit, dressed and cut into serving pieces
1 partridge, plucked, cleaned, and cut into serving pieces
1 mature pheasant, plucked, cleaned, and cut into serving pieces
1 carrot, peeled and sliced in rounds
1 onion, peeled and chopped
¼ teaspoon sage
3 juniper berries
1 bay leaf
2 parsley stems
1 teaspoon fresh or ¼ teaspoon dried thyme
1 cup dry white wine

1. Preheat oven to 400 degrees.

2. Brown the meats, carrot, and onion in a roasting pan in the oven. As each item finishes browning, transfer it to a stock pot.

3. Add sage, juniper berries, bay leaf, parsley stems, and thyme to the stock pot.

4. Pour off excess fat from the browning pan and deglaze it rapidly with the white wine: Pour the wine into the pan, bring to a boil over medium heat, and scrape loose as much of the meat drippings as you can from the bottom of the pan, incorporating them into the wine. Pour all liquid into the stock pot. Add 1 cup of water. Then reduce liquid to a glaze (until it has evaporated and started to caramelize). Immediately add enough cold water to cover the ingredients. Bring to a boil, skim thoroughly, reduce heat and simmer, uncovered, for 3 hours. Add water, if necessary, to keep up the level.

5. Remove large solid ingredients. Strain the stock through a chinois. Let cool without completely covering.

6. Refrigerate. When the stock has solidified, remove the layer of fat that has formed at the top. Then heat the stock gently to liquefy it. Pour it into small containers and freeze.

MAKES APPROXIMATELY 5 QUARTS

❦ MARINADES

A. RAW MARINADE FOR ORDINARY MEAT OR SMALL CUTS OF GAME

1 small carrot, peeled and sliced in rounds
1 small onion, peeled and thinly sliced
2 shallots, peeled and chopped
1 tablespoon chopped celery
1 clove garlic, put through a press
1 sprig fresh or ¼ teaspoon dried thyme
½ bay leaf
3 whole black peppercorns
1 clove
2½ cups dry white wine
1 cup vinegar
½ cup oil

B. RAW MARINADE FOR MAJOR CUTS OF GAME

Double all solid ingredients for Marinade A, add 1 teaspoon fresh or ¼ teaspoon dried rosemary, and increase oil to 1¾ cups and vinegar to 6½ cups. Eliminate white wine.

C. COOKED MARINADE FOR GIGOT EN CHEVREUIL (page 63)

Triple all solid ingredients for Marinade A. In addition, use 10 fresh or dried juniper berries plus 2 teaspoons each fresh or ¼ teaspoon each dried basil and rosemary. Use 7½ cups dry white wine, 2¼ cups vinegar, and 2 cups oil.

Heat the oil until a sprig of parsley will sizzle in it. Then add all solid ingredients and brown lightly. At this point, pour in the wine and vinegar. Bring to a boil, reduce heat and simmer slowly for 30 minutes. Let cool.

❧ SAUCE TOMATE

1 ounce (about 1 tablespoon) diced bacon
2 tablespoons butter
1 small carrot, peeled and finely diced
1 small onion, peeled and finely diced
1 bay leaf, crumbled
1 sprig fresh or 1/4 teaspoon dried thyme
3 pounds fresh tomatoes or canned Italian tomatoes, seeded and
    chopped
1¾ cups chicken stock, homemade (page 122) or canned
1 small clove garlic, peeled and crushed
1 tablespoon sugar
1 tablespoon salt
1 pinch pepper

1. Blanch the bacon in simmering water for 10 minutes. Drain.
2. Preheat oven to 300 degrees.
3. In a small skillet, brown the bacon lightly in the butter. Then add the carrot, onion, bay leaf, and thyme. Sauté until onions have turned golden. Transfer to a heavy, nonaluminum pot.
4. Add all remaining ingredients. Bring to a boil, stirring. Cover and cook in oven for 3 hours.
5. Push through a chinois. Let cool. Freeze in small containers.

MAKES ABOUT 2 CUPS

❧ SAUCE VINAIGRETTE

Stir together 3 parts peanut oil and 1 part vinegar or lemon juice. Season with salt, pepper, and Dijon mustard. I like to crush 3 cloves of garlic and stir them into 1 cup of sauce. Either way, with or without garlic, vinaigrette is *the* salad dressing. It does interfere with the degustation of fine wines, which is why salad comes late in a French meal. Some connoisseurs try to soften the blow to the palate by using walnut oil for vinaigrette. Frankly, I am quite content to cleanse my palate with a glass of water and then take more wine with cheese or dessert. On those rare occasions when I find myself serving a truly great wine at the end of dinner, I eliminate salad altogether.

On most days, the pleasure of a good vinaigrette should not be forgone. Mix it up fresh just before dinner. Then stir it again before serving, since it separates quickly. Pour it over the salad at the last minute and toss.

SAUCE RAVIGOTE

Sauce Ravigote is an interesting variation on vinaigrette. To 1 cup of the basic sauce, add 2 teaspoons drained capers, 1 tablespoon very finely chopped onion, 1 tablespoon finely chopped parsley, and 1 tablespoon of chopped, mixed fresh herbs: chervil, tarragon, and chive. Serve with cold meats, chicken, vegetables, calf's head and feet, lamb's trotters. Stir well. Add more of your favorite ingredient, if you like, since the basic vinaigrette is only meant as a vehicle for the capers and herbs.

Index

C

A Note about the Author

RAYMOND SOKOLOV was born in Detroit in 1941. He graduated from Harvard, then attended Wadham College, Oxford, as a Fulbright Scholar before returning to Harvard for graduate study. He has worked as a foreign correspondent and book critic for *Newsweek* and as the Food Editor for *The New York Times*. Mr. Sokolov wrote a monthly feature for *Natural History* magazine for twenty years. And for the past fourteen years he has been the Leisure & Arts Editor for *The Wall Street Journal*. He lives with his wife in New York City.

A Note on the Type

The text of this book was set in Intertype Garamond, a modern rendering of the type first cut by Claude Garamond (1510–1561). Garamond was a pupil of Geoffroy Tory and is believed to have based his letters on the Venetian models, although he introduced a number of important differences, and it is to him we owe the letter which we know as old-style. He gave to his letters a certain elegance and a feeling of movement that won for their creator an immediate reputation and the patronage of Francis I of France.